5,000 MILES IN A CATAMARAN

5,000 miles
in a
CATAMARAN

Ralph Stephenson

ROBERT HALE & COMPANY · LONDON

© Ralph Stephenson 1974
First published in Great Britain 1974

ISBN 0 7091 4689 2

Robert Hale & Company
63 Old Brompton Road
London SW7

910.45
2

Ro

Made and printed in Great Britain by
The Garden City Press Limited,
Letchworth, Hertfordshire SG6 1JS

35895

CONTENTS

ILLUSTRATIONS

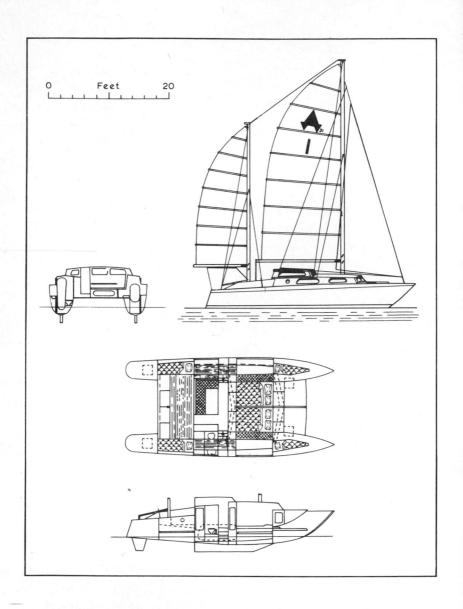

Pussy Cat as sailed by the author. LOA 35 feet; DWL 28 feet;
beam 16 feet; draft 2 feet 6 inches; SA 600 square feet.

FOREWORD

This book is an account of a number of cruises and the incidents, adventures and places they led to. Included as a matter of interest, are occasional discussions of general matters connected with sailing. These express the personal opinions of an average amateur sailor with no claim to be an expert or authority. Indeed much of the book is a tale of difficulty and misfortune. But it is hoped that it expresses also some of the joy of sailing, and that it will encourage others to go and do better.

Ralph Stephenson

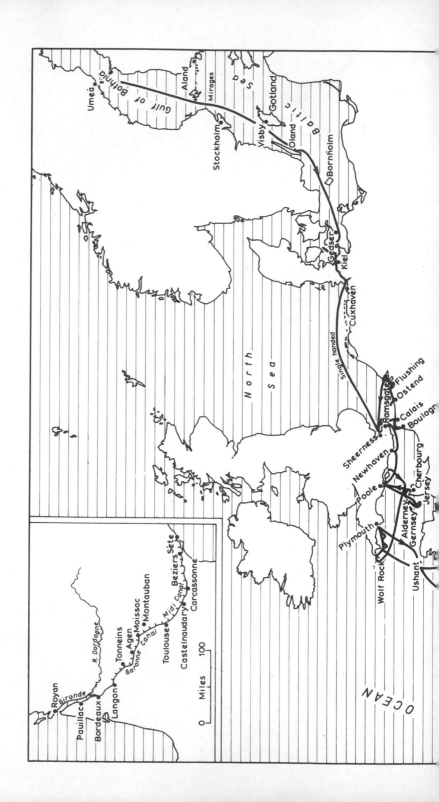

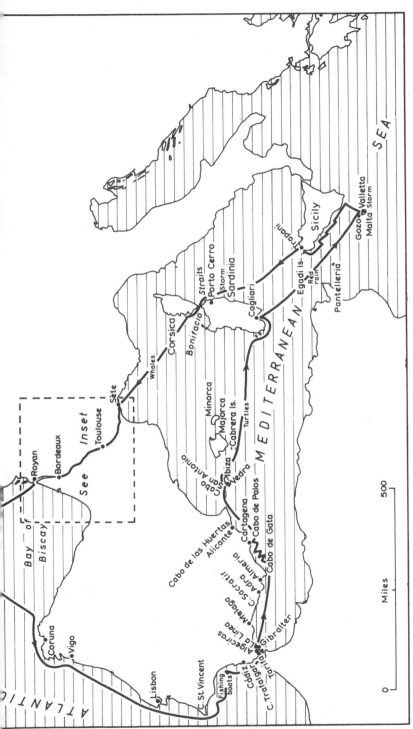

Voyages of the *Pussy Cat*

The Owl and the Pussy-Cat went to sea

- Edward Lear

When men come to like a sea-life they are not fit to live on land.

- Samuel Johnson

CHAPTER ONE

SMALL BOATS ABROAD

From earth' s wide bounds, from ocean's farthest coast
- W.W. How

I started on the water in Hong Kong in 1936. For a year, two of
us shared a clinker-built lifeboat, powered by an old Ford
engine which had been adapted (the word 'marinised' had yet
to be coined) by a local mechanic. Then growing tired both of
the engine's frequent breakdowns and its ear-shattering noise
and vibration when in action, and impressed by the quiet and
grace of the numerous sailing boats which glided past us, I
sold my share and bought a Y-class 18ft racer and day-sailer.

I learned to sail quite quickly on this boat by taking her out
alone on the day I bought her. It was all due to a misunder-
standing, with the boat-boy Ah Lung, who sailed the vessel
round to the town pier, and assuming I wouldn't have been
fool enough to buy a boat unless I knew something about
sailing, handed me the tiller.

'Go ashore and cast off the bow,' I told him. That was what
we used to do in the motor boat. 'I'll try to sail her, Ah Lung.'

He thought I said *alone* not *Ah Lung,* and that I wanted to
take her out single-handed, which was not the case at all. So
he stayed on the quay, pushed the bow round into the light
off-shore wind then pushed off the stern. The mainsail, with
the boom sheeted about halfway, filled nicely in the beam
wind, and I was somehow able to gather in the jib and steer to
leeward of another yacht that was coming into the pier. Then I
was out in the stream and rippling along with a favourable
tide, and I wouldn't have gone back (even if I could have) for a

hundred pounds. By trial and error and with a couple of gentle
gybes, I found out how to handle her on all points, and by the
time I came back to the yacht harbour four hours later, I
could sail. Fortunately, Ah Lung met me in a dinghy at the
entrance to the crowded basin and took the yacht to her
mooring.

The Y-boat was one of the earlier one-design boats, similar
to a Mylin 18-footer. They used to describe boats in those days
sometimes by the water-line length, and as I remember it, she
was 18ft on the water-line and perhaps 24ft overall. She was
much earlier than the popular Dragon boat, which was then
the predominant class yacht locally. The Dragon boat (which
incidentally then sold for a long-forgotten £120) with its
daring Bermudian rig and greater overall length of 29ft, could
point higher and invariably did better in races, but the Y-boat
was a fair match for a Dragon on a reach or running. Y-boats
had pretty big overhangs fore and aft and a central cockpit
where the crew sat on the floor or on low seats. There was a
stumpy mast, but the mainsail had, besides a long boom, a tall
gaff which was pulled up vertical to increase the luff of the
mainsail almost by twice the height of the mast. The short
mast meant a reduced height for the fore-triangle, but its area
was increased by an extended foot made possible by a short
bowsprit.

With a deep, short, fixed lead keel and a large rudder
behind it, she went about easily in stays, and in an emergency
could turn on a sixpence. She would ghost along in light airs,
handle easily under jib or main alone, and I cannot recall
missing the help of an engine. True, with short-distance,
weekend and day sailing, one took care to go and come back
with favourable tides. I used to race her in the class events, but
what I remember most are the single-handed, cruising week-
ends, camping with a lilo and a primus-stove under an awning
in the cockpit. There, in a quiet sunlit cove, with clear water
and sandy bottom one had the world pretty well to oneself,
and it was hard to think that the noise and bustle, the stink

and misery of one of the world's largest, richest and poorest
cities were only a few miles away. There was always fish to be
bought from the local boatmen, and the water was a permanent invitation to dive in.

After a few years the cruising side won the day, and I sold
my Y-12 (she never had any other name) for a tiny cruiser
called *Psyche*. She was only about the same overall length, but
she had a real cabin with a fixed berth to port and a
pipe-berth to starboard. She had been designed by a
Sparkman and Steven's representative who had come from
New York to the Far East on more important business -
namely to investigate the possibility of using the skill and low
cost of the local ship-building yards to produce yachts for
the American market. I took her over when she was halfway
through being built by a Chinese yard for the now unbeliev-
able sum of £45. But even at £45 she wasn't such a good buy.
A far cry from the famous firm's America Cup winners,
perhaps *Psyche*'s line had been drawn on the back of a menu
after an over-generous dinner. She had a short, stubby bow
that butted into the sea and lost way in even the mildest chop.
She was heavy and awkward, and her Bermudian rig was less
efficient than Y-12's old-fashioned gaff. This was a lesson not
to prefer accommodation to sailing qualities; perhaps also
a lesson to stick to the well-tried production model rather than
the problematical one-off-the-cuff. However, the lessons were
not to last long, for my enjoyment of *Psyche*, like Sparkman
and Steven's Far Eastern project, was interrupted by Japanese
invasion.

I have indicated that, at the knock-down prices prevailing,
yachting in pre-war Hong Kong was not a rich man's privilege.
But in that unreal, imperial dream-world, even poor men were
rich men. In some ways it made everything too easy. One was
cut off from some of the basic and enjoyable skills and chores
of mucking about in boats, and though I owned three vessels
and sailed there for five years, my apprenticeship in many
aspects of looking after small boats, didn't begin until I

returned to England many years later.

In fact sailing was often less an opportunity for do-it-yourself than the status symbol of a ruling caste. One was never bothered by practical details of maintenance - bilges, rigging, sails, toilets, cookers, batteries, engines. Every boat owner had a 'yacht boy' (sometimes several) and 'master' left everything to him or to the yard. The boy would do all the cleaning and maintenance, arrange repairs, replacements, slipping, the lot. Master could simply ring up the yard and ask for the boat to be at the pier after lunch on Saturday or Sunday. There, well fortified by gin, he had only to step on board with his guests, and might well spend less time manipulating the sheets and the tiller than the pewter beer-mugs, or the silver stirrup cups. The yacht would be sailed by the crew to a fashionable resort where the guests could bathe. Then an elegant tea would be served and the boat motored home in time for drinks before dinner. If my sailing wasn't quite on that scale, I was still cushioned enough, and what I didn't know about maintenance was almost everything.

One learned more by being a member of the naval volunteers, who foregathered twice a week on a training ship in the harbour, and were solidly grounded in compass work, dead reckoning, rule of the road, morse, semaphore, flags and the rest, by two petty officers and a naval commander. There was attachment to HM ships - an aircraft carrier, destroyers and motor-torpedo boats - as well as our own miscellaneous collection of mine-sweeping trawlers and tugs. Big ships were rather remote from sailing; they were such bewildering mazes of complex machinery, where one could be employed for hours without seeing the sea. But the rest of it was invaluable. Knowing even a little about, say, international code flags, made one appreciate their complexity and the training and experience that goes into a specialised signal officer's job. One learns negatively what is *not* practical on a small boat. At the same time one can pick out the useful scraps - like W flag for 'I require medical assistance', or the hoist ZD2 for 'Please report me at Lloyds'. Even if one isn't good at Morse one has the confidence, after practising with others, to flash a few words slowly and laboriously, and make a fist of reading a reply at the same speed.

In Hong Kong I never got caught out in a storm, or driven ashore, or run down, and, unscathed at its moorings, my Y-boat survived the 1937 typhoon with winds gusting up to 164 miles an hour, which wrecked twenty-seven big ships, from cargo boats to ocean liners, all of them sheltering inside the harbour itself. I spent the nights in port or peacefully at anchor - except for one occasion. I was coming back in the early evening from Rocky Harbour with only a mile or two of open sea to cross before the entrance to the main harbour at Fat Tong Mun, when a soft, grey-white blanket of fog quickly covered land and sea alike, and I might just as well have been a hundred miles offshore. I might have lost my bearings completely, and been wrecked on the rocks to the north and west, for I had no compass on board, but fortunately there was a long, steady swell coming in with the wind from the east. Taking direction from the wind and swell, I hove to on the port tack with the boat moving crabwise a quarter of a knot out to sea, between south-south-east and south by east. Then I hung an oil lamp in the rigging and curled up in the cockpit, looking out every hour or so and devoutly hoping neither the wind nor the swell would change direction. The fog persisted all night, but fortunately no ships came near and the wind stayed steady. In the morning the sun banished the mist in short order, and I was only an hour late for the office. Much later in this story, in hurricane winds off Malta, we backed the jib and hove to on the same port tack to come safely through the night. But this is anticipating.

There was to be no more sailing until after the war, and then I found myself in the Seychelles, one of the most beautiful spots in the world for sailing or underwater fishing. Alas, in the post-war consumer shortage there was no goggle-

fishing gear to be had, nor on the islands was there very much
in the way of cruising yachts. The Seychellois had developed a
clinker-built, centre-board sailing boat, modelled on old
whalers, for the islands had been a resort of whalers and
pirates in the days before any permanent settlement. There
were even rumours of buried treasure and once (rather in the
way one used to be shown dirty postcards) I was furtively
shown and old map, and invited to invest money in a 'dig'.

These locally built, open boats, large cockle-shells, sloop-
rigged and with a fair spread of canvas, sailed well enough,
but they were liable to sudden capsizes and without covered
decks, they were too open to venture far out to sea, even
though the Seychelles Islands were peculiarly favoured in their
weather. They were too far north to be affected by the
hurricanes which periodically devastated Mauritius, and there
were two seasons : the north-east monsoon from November to
April which blew or not as it felt inclined, and the south-west
monsoon from May to October, a much more reliable, steady
Force 3 to 5. Potential hazards in these waters were the
ever-changing coral reefs. You could see them clearly enough
by day, and I never heard of any of the harbour boats coming
to grief, no doubt because of good local knowledge. But the
last of the inter-island schooners, a three-master, and the most
handsome sight imaginable under sail, left her bones piled up
on a reef, while there were fatal landing accidents to the flying
boats stationed in Mahe during and after the war. Certainly
night sailing anywhere close inshore would have been courting
disaster.

So steady was the weather, that the local income-tax
inspector used to commute to the office five days a week by
sailing boat. The only harm he suffered was being caught once
in the rain on his way to the office so that, being a conscien-
tious chap, he worked all day in wet clothes and finished up in
hospital with pneumonia. After that he always kept a change
of clothes in his desk.

The local boats were used for family picnics to the

numerous islands in the harbour, or for Saturday racing. Yacht racing was most popular with the Seychellois, and this too was very much a family affair. It was not unusual to see a crew of say father, mother and three children with a couple of friends to help out, handling the boat like veterans, moving together and almost instinctively from starboard to port, or vice versa, as they went about, shifting slightly aft on a run; and generally doing everything to achieve the best possible balance. They were all used to the water and when a boat capsized, it was quite a sight to see them all -dignified patricians, staid matrons, sloe-eyed youngsters - floating in flowing garments (for they sailed in much the same clothes they wore to church), and again working skilfully and fast to right her, bale her, and get her into the race again. They almost always won, partly because they knew and handled the boats so well, partly because they took good care to keep everything as light as possible, kept their boats dry on shore between Saturdays, and were even said to treat the bottom with boot-polish before a race.

I had a half share in one of these boats and got a great deal of pleasure out of her. Even being becalmed was no hardship, for if it was near a reef, one could look down through the still water, and even without goggles, see traceries and flowers of bright-coloured coral, and the dozens of brilliant, darting fish slipping through the branches.

I made only one longish passage, from the main island, Mahe, to Praslin, the home of the unique coco-de-mer. This strange fruit, three times as large as a coconut and taking seven years to ripen, is said by some to be the 'forbidden fruit' of the Bible and the valley of the Coco-de-mer, the original Garden of Eden. There was no need to sail by the tide, and being on a tour of inspection, I started off at eight o'clock on Monday morning. The distance was thirty miles, only slightly more than from Dover to Calais, and I made the crossing in eight-and-a-half hours with a light beam wind (it was the south-west monsoon) all the way. Once out at sea there was a

long, slow swell with waves maybe five to seven feet high. With
only a suggestion of land on the horizon and, despite the
steadiness of the weather, I felt, in a completely undecked
boat, extremely exposed, rather like one of those three wise
men of Gotham who went to sea in a bowl. And yet in not very
different craft, castaways and shipwrecked mariners have
covered thousands of miles.

CHAPTER TWO

HOME WATERS

Then the bowsprit got mixed with the rudder sometimes.
- Hunting of the Snark

There was fine goggle-fishing but little sailing in Ghana and Sierra Leone where I spent the fifties, and my sea time really began again, after I had settled in England, with a calamitous family sailing holiday in Salcombe. We picked the wettest and coldest August weather of the decade, if not of the century, and although it had an appropriately nautical name and the attractive address of Shadycombe Creek, the boat-hire firm was anything but efficient. We were to have a spacious house-boat moored in the beautiful estuary, a 15ft Trident sail-boat, and a dinghy - all of them on hire for a week.

The hire began from noon, and we arrived, all five of us (Jane, David, Jonny, Camilla and Ralph), at two in the afternoon, having foolishly gone without lunch in our eager-ness to get afloat. Alas, Bill the boatman was away on a job in the only motor-boat which could take us out to our mooring, and though he was expected every moment, he didn't turn up until 4.45 pm. We loaded our bags in the rain and set out. Across the harbour, round the point, up an arm of the estuary we went, and as the rain-sodden journey stretched from twenty to thirty minutes, I began to wonder.

'Do we have to row all this way whenever we want to go to town - to any shops?' I asked wetly.

'Oh. It ernt so far, said Bill with a reassuring West country burr. 'Not if you pick the tide.'

The house-boat turned out to be a clapped-out five-tonner

moored fore and aft. The mast had been taken out and some
concrete poured into the bilges. She had four exiguous bunks
(Camilla then ten had to sleep on the cabin floor where we all
tripped over her), a two-burner gas stove, a basin and a bucket
for washing, and a loo that didn't work. The 15ft Trident had
one of the rigging-screws on its rusting shrouds replaced by
nylon cord, and weed grew a good six inches on the bottom.
We looked for a place to haul her out, but there was mud for
miles, and though we did our best to scrub her in the water, the
local wits made shear-like motions with their fingers when we
crawled past, and one brave fellow asked if we would like to
borrow a lawn-mower. Apart from being old and as heavy as
lead, the dinghy seemed all right, except that when we'd rowed
in to buy the inevitably-forgotten items of stores (a good
hour-and-a-half it took) and were on our way back, one of the
oars unaccountably snapped. I've never broken an oar before
or since, so I must have been feeling strongly about the
situation. Fortunately we were near the boat-yard and after
some 'arnt-ing' and 'ernt-ing' and I will say good-humoured
West country burr-ing, we got another (I won't say new) oar.

We lurched from disaster to disaster. Dropped things
overboard, because there were too many of us and not enough
room. There was no sun. It drizzled intermittently, the wind
was fitful or failed entirely, and the water was freezing cold.
We went aground on the mud. We muddled up the tides so as
to find ourselves at dusk, five miles from base, no wind, and
with two hours to go before the tide turned in our favour. The
climax came near the end of the week when we set off for the
day and sailed right down to the entrance, towing the dinghy
behind the Trident. For once the sun was shining, there was a
moderate breeze and the tide helped us along. At lunch-time
we reached a quiet beach, just to the east of the entrance,
anchored the Trident and rowed ashore to swim and picnic on
the sands, keeping a careful eye on the mother-ship, bobbing
up and down, giving the world an occasional skittish glimpse
of her bottom, still a patchy green despite diligent scrubbing.

After lunch it was agreed that David and I would take the sailing-boat unencumbered by the dinghy and try out her paces, while Jane, Jonny and Camilla, would stay on the beach. Then when we got back they would row out to join us for the long voyage home.

The breeze was still steady, and in one long tack we were through the twin headlands of Bolt Head and Lambury Point and out to sea. I wasn't sure if this was inside the charter limits, but nothing had been said and I felt much happier than in the shallows round the house-boat. It was exhilarating reaching along the coast with a steadily freshening beam wind, and we went further than I had intended. It was after 1600 hours when we got back in the vicinity of the beach. Still the wind was well in our favour and we should make good time back to our base. However, the peaceful beach was transformed into a mass of white horses. They were middle-sized waves rather than great crashing breakers, and would have been nothing to the life-guards on the Sydney beach, but when Jane, Jonny and Camilla tried to row out to us, one wave larger than the rest, caught them sideways and capsized the dinghy. Jonny, wearing a life-jacket, swam to some nearby rocks. David got overboard in his bathing-suit and waded through the surf to help. Numerous bathers, swimmers, waders and other aquatic holidaymakers, helped Jane and Camilla (who were in their only clothes and soaking wet) to right the dinghy, bale it out and get them on their way again through the surf, this time successfully.

But I was soon in trouble. I had been sailing up and down just beyond the surf waiting for them to come alongside, when suddenly the helm jammed. A frantic inspection showed that the eye holding the upper pintle of the rudder had come adrift. It had been loose but no worse than all the rest of the gear, and one had hoped. . . With a couple of the right-sized bolts it could have been fixed in ten minutes. As it was. . . I unshipped the rudder and immediately the eye fell into the sea. That was that.

The Trident had been banging about in the wind and the wet rowers in the dinghy were getting impatient. I waved and shouted to them.

'The rudder's broken. I can't control this boat properly. You'll have to row home.' I could see they were all right now, and it would have been foolish to try and transfer anyone from the dinghy to a sailing-boat without a rudder, even if we could have managed it. Fortunately the mast was stepped well forward, and with the wind astern she held a reasonably steady course in the direction I wanted to go. I could even control her by putting my weight on one side or the other, or more drastically by gybing. With my teeth clenched, eyes everywhere and boat-hook metaphorically at the ready (there wasn't actually one in the inventory), I proceeded down the narrow estuary at what seemed to me a breakneck speed through a veritable armada of launches, ferries, outboards, motor-sailers, small boats and at least two dinghy races.

All the same I had the better part of it. Though it was nervous work, I was able to sail right up to our house-boat in about an hour, and at least I was dry. The others, huddled together in the dinghy, took turns at rowing until they reached the town side of the estuary. There Jane, with Jonny and Camilla, insisted on being put ashore at the first possible landing-place, perhaps because she thought there were too many for the dinghy, or that it would be quicker walking or more comfortable out of the wind, or perhaps because she'd had enough of boats. Unfortunately, the first possible landing-place was the garden of Salcombe's smartest and most luxurious hotel, and before they came to the road, they had to make their way, dripping with water and apologies, through lounges and bars, past couples politely sipping tea, past scornful-looking receptionists and hall-porters. Then they had a considerable walk before they met up with David again, and had to row the last lap to the house-boat in the dark. I had hot tea and drinks ready, and after a large meal and a lot of drying-out, we went to bed and slept soundly in the comforting knowledge that next day we could honourably give up and return to London and hot baths, and be able to talk vaguely and airily about 'our sailing holiday in Salcombe'.

Salcombe is not my lucky spot for on a later West country cruise, we spent the night there and found it very crowded and noisy with the sound of transistor radios and outboard engines floating across the water until dawn. I was in a chartered trimaran, and Salcombe was not lucky for the boat either. The following year the owner, sailing her in the Crystal Trophy Race, and taking shelter from southerly gales, was pooped at the entrance to Salcombe, the boat swept broadside on by a wave, and his son (fortunately wearing a life-jacket and soon picked up) swept overboard. A monohull following behind him was dismasted. It is another demonstration, if one were needed, that close quarters and shoal waters can be the most dangerous of all. But all this belongs to the next episode but one.

Perhaps as a result of Salcombe, the family because somewhat unenthusiastic about sailing, though they all came to see my various boats, and came out generally on fairly short passages. Three of them suffer from mal-de-mer and David, the best sailor, having a young family himself, can't very well desert them for long cruises. As a result I've sailed sometimes single-handed, sometimes with friends male or female, and when I got *Pussy Cat,* with a crew paying or sharing expenses. There is more to say of owners and crews later, but here let me say I haven't regretted any of it. It is good to have done some single-handed sailing, if only to appreciate the toughness, skill and spirit of the real stunt-men. At the same time, in company the pleasure of sailing is multiplied by being shared. Unsuccessful mixtures or temperamental behaviour hardly seem to exist at sea. The phrase 'all in the same boat' is a deep-seated truth. One immediately gets to know men and women on friendly terms, and because of the mutual dependence, to appreciate them, to rely on them, and invariably to respect them. At the same time, one doesn't get to know them too

well. A small boat at sea isn't a boudoir. Sailing takes the heat
out of sex, and like many sports and outdoor activities, it is an
opportunity for men and women to meet as human beings as
well as members of the opposite sex. Marriage is another
matter, and I've nothing but admiration for the several
couples who write about sailing, and the innumerable others
whose boat is their home. It proves the toughness of the
institution. If people can live and sail together summer and
winter alike, they have a bond that is not only proof against
human weakness, but is wind, water and weather resistant as
well. For the majority there is the pleasure of banding together
for a common purpose, and then when the journey's end is
achieved going back to family or friends.

My next cruises were in three and four-tonners, chartered
from a boat-hire firm in Chichester. This was an excellent
firm, and a member of the Yacht Charterers' Association, a
group that sets high standards for charter yachts, hoping to
influence the market and drive out of business firms with such
slipshod methods and hiring such unseaworthy craft, as we had
suffered from in Salcombe. This firm's boats were carefully
fitted out, checked between hires, well equipped for coastal
and later cross-channel cruising, and all the gear was in sound
condition. There was a fixed agreement about cruising limits,
insurance, liability for loss, damage or delay. Before hiring
they asked about experience; before setting sail, they came on
board and spent an hour explaining how to start the engine,
pump the bilges, light the stove, and carefully went over the
inventory.

The boats themselves were not very new (I remember a
Meteor one-design with cabin added called *Mariposa)*, not
very big (21 to 23ft length overall), not very fast, and not very
comfortable (no standing headroom, and only one of them had
a loo). But they were cheap to hire and you could take the
whole boat for a week at not more than £5 a day. The firm has
deservedly flourished and nowadays they hire 30 to 35-footers

(Excalibur, Bonito, Pioneer) but their charges have increased in proportion. I went out from Chichester in these boats five years running from 1963 to 1967 - single-handed a couple of times, once with David and twice with Elizabeth, a friend of long-standing who liked sailing.

The 1963 holiday was a shakedown cruise, mucking about Chichester Harbour, sailing outside for a day, going across to Bembridge and back. In 1964 I set off on a Saturday in September. I was alone, mainly because we had already had a family holiday, and the schools had started again. Jane and Camilla came out for a sail from Hayling Island as I was on my way out of Chichester Harbour, which meant some nippy work with the dinghy, as the tides in and out of the entrance are strong. I spent the night at Wootton Creek in the Solent and discovered in the morning my watch had stopped. I had no radio on board and none of the boats had echo-sounding, so I had to calculate the tides as best I could by estimating the time, and using a lead and line. It proved to be not very efficient.

On Sunday I made good time through the Solent with a fair tide, passed Yarmouth at 1300 hours and decided to go on to Poole. The only pilot on board was Coles' *Creeks and Harbours of the Solent,* which did not cover Poole, but I had a Stanton chart of the coast with a little inset plan of Poole Harbour. I had times of high water at Dover and tidal differences for the Solent, but not Poole. I thought I could work out a tide difference and didn't realise how inadequate this was to cope with the complex tides in Poole Harbour. I beat through the North Channel and across the Bay, then in past the Sandbanks ferry with a flood tide. In the growing dark I found the channel confusing, with the number of boats moored either side, and anchored north of it in what I hoped was enough water. About 0400 hours my hopes were dashed. *Mariposa* heeled gradually over as she dried out; I rolled steadily off my bunk on to the side of the boat, and the bilge water crept slowly into my sleeping-bag. . . In Monday morning sunshine, a damp sleeping-bag drying on the cabin-top, I motored up to the town quay for shopping, then on round Brownsea Island and Green Island making for the entrance again and, hopefully, a passage to Weymouth. But I never got there.

I lost track of the stakes marking the channel, went aground in the mud, pushed off again. Then near the entrance some time after noon - where was the next port-hand buoy? The outgoing tide was carrying me faster than I intended - where was it? Suddenly there was a gentle grating under the keel, and the boat felt more *solid*. The water was flowing past her. I got out and tried to push her off. I might just as well have tried to push the *Queen Mary*. Soon she was high and dry, and as she lay on her side I could walk all round her and go digging for clams or build sand-castles, if I felt so inclined. I pored over the tiny harbour plan and stared at the patch near the entrance. Was there a line under that 5? Yes, there might be. It was really too small to see. A magnifying glass was another of the essentials for good navigation I didn't happen to have. It seemed I was there till the next high tide, whenever that was. A passing launch said 1500 hours. But the afternoon came and went, the sea came and went no higher than when I had gone aground. At dusk some men with forks came to dig for bait. 'It's the second high tide you want,' they explained. 'Between ten and eleven tonight.'

They lent me a spare fork to dig a channel under the keel, and I laid out a kedge anchor ready to pull her off. As it got dark I mentally noted a large catamaran that had floated all day at her moorings and thought I would anchor near her. By about 2130 hours my boat was free. I got the engine going, hauled in the anchor and motored over and anchored near the catamaran. But at 0500 hours (horrors!) I heeled over aground again, though this time only for half an hour. Perhaps I hadn't gone near enough to the other boat, perhaps though only half the size, *Mariposa* drew more than the catamaran. Tuesday I decided would be an easy day, sailing south to Anvil Point, and though I missed the tide returning and took thirty minutes to cover a measured mile, I got back before dark. I anchored in almost the same place, but this time, after careful sounding, on the deeper side of the catamaran and in plenty of water, though it was low tide. Blow me down, at dawn I was aground again! The boat had swung round on her anchor cable into shallower water.

As a result, on Wednesday instead of getting under way by 0600 hours I had to wait until 0730 hours, but I hadn't missed the tide, and carried it all the way back by the North Channel into the Solent to Newtown River. There I was back with more book information about tides, I firmly picked up a vacant buoy marked *Dolcibella,* and after much sounding and worry, decided I would float at low tide. On Thursday the engine wouldn't start, but I got out under the jib and had a fine sail up to Southampton docks and the big liners. Then, coming back to Yarmouth, the wind got up worse and worse. I reefed the main to ease the poor labouring creature, then got soaked changing to a smaller jib since the big one was getting a bashing. Going into Yarmouth without an engine was tricky, but I managed to tack up between the rows of yachts, tied up alongside on the outside of the outside row, and even managed to get a local mechanic to fix the engine. But at 1900 hours that evening I was aground again! Being fourth boat in line I was moored too far off the channel. When I floated within the hour, I moved a couple of places along where I was third in line, and had no more trouble.

Friday was my last day, and I set off at dawn round the Isle of Wight. Down to the Needles with wind, tide and engine all contributing, I covered the first seven miles in less than an hour, the best speed of the cruise. But the rest of the day, with wind light and variable, was more average. I missed the tide outside Chichester when the wind and the engine both failed, but then a fresh westerly sprang up, and took me comfortably home, home, home.

I mention this cruise in some detail as it was a salutary

lesson on the central feature of sailing in Britain - tides. There were tides in Hong Kong, but nowhere near so strong or with such a rise and fall, and the water was mostly so clear that you could *see* what the depth was. In the Mediterranean tides are negligible, and my Swedish friends from the Baltic asked shyly (or was it slyly?) 'And how about tides? You have that in England, isn't it?'

The first essential on a boat is a book of tide tables. *Admiralty Tide Tables* are the best, and some years later, on another cruise I was able (admittedly with considerable interpolation) to work out within a few minutes when the tide would turn against us going down the Garonne and Gironde from Bordeaux to Royan, and when it would be in our favour again. Also good is *Reed's Almanac* which gives daily tides for all the main British ports and Continental ports from Brest to Cuxhaven, with tidal differences for secondary ports. The Admiralty tables (like the British Navy) are built for efficiency. The information is concise, clear, consistent, compressed and yet completely adequate. Reed's is more like a father figure (Father Neptune or Father Thames perhaps) who enjoys yarning away a bit with such information as: 'The ancient Greek philosophers had little first-hand knowledge of the tides', and 'Tidal streams are a horizontal oscillation of the particles of water'. An endless source of entertainment as well as information, Reed's is half a dozen books rolled into one.

As well as the times of tides, one needs to know the tidal streams. This information is best given diagrammatically. Reed's has many excellent little maps, the Admiralty publish tidal stream atlases which cost very little, and some yachting charts, Stanton's for example, show tidal streams as insets. Since the information relates to high tide at a given place, it is valid from year to year and does not go out of date. The rate of current may vary from half a knot to a formidable ten knots in the Pentland Firth and the Alderney Race. One meets sailing people who say airily, 'Oh I never bother about tides', but I have never had a boat, even a multihull in which one could afford to ignore tidal streams. It is only in speed-boats, which use so much petrol that another ten or twelve gallons is neither here nor there, that one can afford to go roaring off in any direction at any time.

For British coastal waters I would rank an echo-sounder as the most important piece of equipment next to the compass. It is difficult to take hand soundings under way from the narrow decks of a small yacht, and single-handed it is virtually impossible. Echo-sounders seem to be thoroughly reliable compared with most machinery in boats, and they give such a rapid, continuous series of soundings, that it is often possible to feel one's way slowly and cautiously along an unknown channel. An echo-sounder is fine if you are tacking inshore (especially hugging the coast to avoid a foul tide), and although many yacht models only go to fifty fathoms which is a limitation, a check with a sounding on the chart may be a blessing in fog or at night or as confirmation of a cross bearing or recognition of a landmark.

The following year I covered much the same ground (or much the same sea), this time with less wear and tear and no trouble until near the end of the cruise. I had David as crew, I had a better chart of Poole Harbour, and proper tide tables. The only variation on the previous year was going up the Beaulieu River, and it was a new charm, akin to the charm of canal cruising, to sail or motor under forest trees and through grassy meadows.

The trouble came on the last day, on our way back to Chichester, when going across from the Solent, it blew up from the east, and we were bumping up and down close-hauled. The only way of carrying a dinghy in these small yachts was to tow it astern, and the dinghy itself was a fairly heavy plastic pram, rather like a shallow dish. Mostly it trailed along behind happily enough, but in these conditions it kept taking spray aboard and gradually filling with water. We tried a long tow, a medium tow and a short tow, and twice hauled it

up to the yacht, and managed to tip out most of the water.
Finally, after a blustery spell during which our attention was
on the yacht and the weather, we looked round and it wasn't
there. It had gone on its own cruise, taking with it the painter
and a solid cleat which it had pulled free from the counter of the
yacht. We came about and sailed up and down for half-an-
hour, scanning the white horses in all directions, but the
dinghy had vanished. Very likely it was awash and almost
impossible to see.

In 1966 I thought I knew it all, and invited Elizabeth for a
cruise in the Solent. We did well enough except for mistaking
the time by an hour, and as a result going aground on a falling
tide in the narrow, winding Bembridge channel when passing
another yacht. So we spent twelve hours more than we meant
to in Bembridge. Again we went up the Beaulieu River. We
had baths at an hotel, then an elegant dinner in the Master
Builder's House at Buckler's Hard. It was an appropriately
nautical setting, for they used the trees in the forest to build
big ships at Buckler's Hard before the days of steam and iron,
then floated them down the river, and the Master Builder was
a Master *Ship*builder.

But again, despite my vast experience, disaster overtook us
in the end. Coming back on the dot on Friday afternoon, the
day before the hire ended, we had it rough again across from
the Solent Forts to the Chichester entrance. Again the pram
dinghy began to fill with water. This time I had it tied up so it
couldn't break loose, and twice I managed to tip water out of
it. But the bar at the Chichester entrance looked quite nasty, I
had to tack in, and I took my attention off the dinghy long
enough for it to fill with water and sink.The yacht herself, like
a mother being dragged back by a fractious child, lost way,
wouldn't sail close-hauled or go about, and we began to make
leeway on to a sandbank to the west of the entrance. We tried
to pull the dinghy out and tip out the water, but it was like
playing tug-of-war with an elephant.

'What's the dinghy worth?' asked Elizabeth.

'It's not worth as much as the yacht,' I replied. And I untied the painter and let the little brute go. Within seconds we were back on course, and within minutes were inside the harbour. It was difficult to explain just why I had come back from a second cruise minus a dinghy, but this time fortunately she was washed ashore and recovered by the coastguard, and in the end the repairs cost me less than £8.

My last cruise from Chichester (again with Elizabeth but this time with a rubber dinghy) was across to Cherbourg in 1967. For a first Channel crossing we had ideal weather, and except for a calm patch at the start, were reaching all the way with a fresh breeze from the east. We left in the afternoon and it took us nearly until dark to get away from St Catherine's Point, the southerly point of the Isle of Wight. However, this was all to the good as it simplified the navigation. The distance across the Channel is about sixty miles, but at night St Catherine's light is visible for sixteen miles and Cap Bafleur light on the French side for twenty-two miles. Thus the effective crossing during which one is out of sight of any landmark is reduced to twenty miles. In daylight the land is not visible nearly so far off, so that it is easier to cross the Channel by night than by day. About 0300 hours we picked up the Cap Bafleur light winking away every ten seconds. We lost the light at dawn before the coast was visible, and when we did sight land it wasn't easy to identify. However, it wasn't hard to decide that we were east of Cherbourg, and then we picked up a buoy that put us slightly east of Cap Levi. It was fortunate that the easterly wind held steady for the tide running along the coast against us was so strong that we spent a couple of hours sailing hard to stay in the same place. The engine was giving trouble again and unable to lend us a hand. Finally the tide eased and soon we were in sight of the long breakwater and the hills behind the town of Cherbourg. As we got into Cherbourg the wind was gusting wildly, but it was still on the beam and took us easily into the inner yacht harbour under jib alone. We were there by 1300 hours, having made some seventy miles in twenty-one hours.

Of all the pleasure of sailing in England, crossing the Channel in a small boat must be one of the greatest, and one enjoyed by thousands of people every year. The yachtsman becomes more than a mere holidaymaker, almost an ambass-ador, taking a little bit of England to a foreign land. All the ceremony of customs and right of entry, are put in motion for his benefit. Carefully documented, the yacht attains almost diplomatic significance. *Nom, pavillon, porte d'attache, provenance, longeur, largeur* etc. are all entered in his official green card. And having fulfilled his obligations, he enjoys the long-standing privilege of thirsty travellers - duty-free drink and cigarettes. Not to mention, in the case of Cherbourg, *maquereau à la crème* in a quayside restaurant, a dish I still remember to this day.

One enjoys, too, as with all foreign travel, the slight difference in approach in emphasis, in the way of doing things, in the design and appearance of familiar objects - traffic lights, shop fronts, telephone boxes, policemen, bus stops. I had already seen a marina, in 1939 in San Francisco, without quite knowing what it was. But Cherbourg was the first one I had used. It was crowded (not so crowded as I suppose it now is in August) but the floating stages, with long gangways to accommodate the wide range of tide (nearly up to twenty feet at highest springs), provided for an astonishing number of boats.

Perhaps because we came in under sail without an engine, a Frenchman came forward to help us as we nosed up to one of the rows.

'You can take this berth 'ere,' he said, 'The owner is away. 'E won't be back for some time. We know 'im 'ere. 'E is called Eric Tabarly.'

CHAPTER THREE

MONOHULL TO MULTIHULL

But what is this. . .
That so bedeck'd ornate and gay
Comes this way sailing. . .
With all her bravery on and tackle trim
Sails filled and streamers waving. . .

- Milton

It was about this time that, through Elizabeth, I met Tony, a
London doctor who was also keen on sailing. He had recently
bought a trimaran, a Triune, *Sophie of Mathyns,* built in
Poole by Robin Chatworth Musters. At that time multihulls
were something new, and many people were excited by their
speed and accommodation. Many other claims were made
especially for Arthur Piver's designs, some of them perhaps
with a substantial element of sales talk. 'Trans-ocean tested'
was one slogan I remember. I had read a little more sober
discussion about them in yachting papers and the Amateur
Yacht Research Society's publications, enough to make me
very interested. I heard, too, that Tony's boat 'had everything',
and when he offered to let Elizabeth and me have her on
charter for a week or so in the summer of 1968, I accepted
without hesitation.

We had a week-end cruise in June from Maldon to
Brightlingsea, with five on board, but there was no wind, a lot
of people about, and it was difficult to form an opinion of the
boat. However, when we picked her up at Fowey, in Cornwall,
how spacious and well-equipped she proved to be with all the
things that my 4-tonners hadn't got. For navigation there were
echo-sounder, electric log and radio direction finder. There

was full headroom, water piped to sink and washbasin,
grill-and-oven gas cooker, fluorescent electric light, reliable
engine, rubber dinghy, and three double bunks and a single.

Fowey lies between steep hills and the water is still and
deep. At Polruan, we climbed vertical streets with a bird's-eye
view of boats lying in patterned rows at their moorings.
Upstream a large steamer peered round the side of a hill,
looking in the narrow river like a giant in a dolls' house.
Ashore, drinking beer in the pub, were bearded characters
(one even wore gold earrings) who might have appeared in
Treasure Island. We left Fowey at 1100 hours on Tuesday with
a fine following wind past Black Head, Mevagissy and the
Gwineas Rock Buoy, but lost the breeze off Dodman Point,
lurched about in the swell with no appetite for lunch, and
came into the Falmouth entrance past the neat, white lighthouse and the smugglers' caves near St Anthony's Head,
much later than expected. We went in with a light south-easter
and swung east into St Mawes' crowded bay carrying full sail -
rashly as it turned out for the breeze suddenly blew fresh from
the north as we were hesitating between one attractive
anchorage and another, and we had to pick up a buoy hastily,
much further from the village than we intended. We went for a
walk ashore and explored the smugglers' caves from the land
side. On a coastal cruise one is privileged to be an inhabitant
of two worlds. The only drawback is that the link between
them is often an uncomfortable one - tricky anchorages, long
dinghy trips, wet muddy feet.

On Wednesday we got off to an early start for the north-east
corner of Mounts Bay. A fine running breeze took us down
past the Manacle Rocks, past a second Black Head and round
the Lizard. The lines we put out for mackerel brought their first
catches, as we had fried fish for lunch. Round the corner
the wind was against us. Slowly we beat up the Bay and it was
clear we were not going to arrive before low water. Of three
unknown ports Newlyn seemed a better bet than Mousehole or
Penzance. Mousehole would be dried out completely and we

would be locked out of the inner harbour at Penzance where they shut the gates to keep the water in. So we wound our way into Newlyn among the pilchard fleet, and found enough water and enough room. Newlyn is really a rather dull little commerical port. But it was transformed by the luminous evening light, so that the groups fishing and strolling on the high stone walls looked like characters out of a sea opera, ready to burst into song at the drop of a jib sheet. Also between the grey piers at the entrance, St Michael's Mount was framed fair and square with the evening light about it like a halo. Saint Michael himself might have been there in the clouds ready to fight a sunset-coloured dragon.

On Thursday, with the northerly wind holding, we slipped south, then west for the Scillies. Off Tater Du Point and Guthenbras Point was a fleet of at least twenty-five small fishing boats, many of them hauling in mackerel lines, thick with fish, as fast as winding balls of wool. The wind lighter and now abeam, we slipped past the Runnelstone and set a course for the Scillies, enveloped in our own warm haze. We never saw the Wolf Rock or Lands End or the Longships Light Vessel. Every half-hour or so we could hear the helicopters that run to the Islands, but never caught sight of one. I worried about the visibility and about our landfall. The wind fell away more, but we kept moving and by 1230 hours in a dead calm we were relieved to sight land. Shortly after, dimly through the haze, we made it out to be the south coast of Saint Mary's. The Admiralty chart of the Islands has a view from the south that must have been drawn all of fifty years ago, but though some of the buildings on Peninnis Head seemed to differ, the general contour of the land and the old lighthouse on Saint Agnes, made it unmistakeable. By 1400 hours, under the engine, we picked up the first channel buoy and were soon at anchor in Saint Mary's harbour in eight feet of clear, turquoise water. There was a sprinkling of boats at anchor, but it was quite uncrowded. The greatest influx of people seemed to be when the ferry came in from the mainland in the

morning. But many of those who came in the morning left
again in the afternoon.

On Friday, after shopping in Hugh Town, we motored
across two miles and anchored in the lee of Tresco. The
Scillies have an air of the tropics, but for bathing the water is
still chilly. On Tresco marram grass, blue globe-flowers and
ice-plant mingle with swathes of flaming purple heather and
tropical palms, and deserted sand-hills roll up to the rocky
headlands. We swam and fished and walked among the bright
heather with a spring a foot thick. On Saturday it was time to
start back. Before 0700 hours, at low water, we crept anxiously
through Crow Sound glued to the echo-sounder as it registered
two feet, and heartened by a local work-boat that surged
confidently past, almost thumbing its nose at us. Soon we were
out past Hats Buoy and Watermill Cove, and the north wind
steady as a rock on the beam, a fresh Force 3 to 4, carried us at
a good eight knots or more to pass the Wolf Rock by 1100
hours and the Lizard by 1500 hours. From then on it was a
thresh northward against the wind, the boat banging into
heavier seas, úntil I gave up and motored the last few miles
into the peaceful, enfolding arms of the Helford River. It was
2000 hours before we picked up a friendly buoy, moored at the
entrance to Porthnavas Creek and looking up the river.
Ahead the hills ran down overlapping one another, dark green
against the lighter green of the water, a miniature version of
the Norwegian Fiords or the New Zealand Sounds. No other
anchorage was so quiet and peaceful, none so alone, con-
templative, almost out of the world.

I intended to go on the Yealm River beyond Plymouth. By
now it was Sunday; we had been sailing pretty hard for five
days, and it was easy to lie in until eight o'clock and have a
leisurely breakfast. It was mid-morning before we came out of
the mouth of the Helford to find the wind, what there was of it,
dead against us. My visions of getting to the Yealm vanished,
and after bumping about in Falmouth Bay with only a few
puffs of wind, it seemed we would have to settle for Saint

Mawes. But just as we got to the entrance the wind freshened from the east and we held it for the rest of the day. North we went, past St Anthony's, past Porthmellin Head. In an hour we had cleared Dodman Point and by 1600 hours, with four fresh mackerel in the cockpit, we picked up the tall, striped daymark on Gribbin Head outside Fowey.

We had to get to Poole by the end of the week, and on Monday it was a long haul across the bay to Salcombe, starting with the wind a point free on the port tack, Rame Head dimly seen, then, the wind veering east, forced south until Eddystone showed dimly on the starboard beam. We made long legs out to sea then in again on starboard tacks, picking up first Borough Island, then Bolt Tail, and finally the welcome, jagged, sawtooth outline of Bolt Head. The tide and wind were against us, but the engine took us slowly in, picking out the buoys and following the leading marks, until we found a space to anchor a hundred yards from the town quay. If you like crowds and bustle, if you like company on land and sea, go to Salcombe and swell the throngs that, in August, swarm in the narrow streets, buzz in dinghies and motor-boats round the landing stages, and cut across the harbour from daylight to dark and then to daylight again. When we were there it was Regatta Week and the water was almost hidden from view by the hundreds of snowy sails - little racers swooping in and out among the anchored yachts like white butterflies in a cabbage patch. Salcombe was lovely but ashore and afloat it was packed to the limit.

We spent half the next day stocking up with fuel, water and provisions, and started round the corner to Dartmouth about noon. Past Prawle Point and as far as Start Point, it was dead calm and we kept the engine going, but there was a north wind lurking round the corner. We tacked out north-east away from the Skerries and finally in to pick up the land again with the tower-like daymark outside Dartmouth on Froward Point and the ragged Mewstone below it. Ahead of us, zigzagging into the entrance, was a 50ft, two-masted French schooner, *Marie*

of Saint Malo, a lovely boat, gliding from leg to leg as
smoothly as a ballroom dancer, a weather-beaten Breton, face
as brown as a berry, at the wheel. Again we went in against the
ebb tide, past the lovely wooded cliffs to a fore-and-aft
mooring allocated by the harbour-master.

Perhaps I may digress to say a word about the harbour-
master one meets at different ports. In some places he is
conspicuous by his absence. In others his boat appears as if by
magic in exactly the right spot to meet you. In other ports, like
Ramsgate or Dover or Saint Peter Port, he gives you instructions from a tower as you go in, or from the sea-wall. In the
Scillies he was cheerful and friendly with a strong West
country accent. 'That Irish boat now (he pointed to a large
ketch with a green-white-and-orange flag) came in for a few
days, but she's been here three months with engine trouble.
Plenty to do, you're right there. When I finish collecting dues I
do a shift as mechanic for the shipping company. Then after
dinner I go off to work on the farm.' Afterwards I saw him out
of his harbour-master's uniform and wearing a boiler suit.
   'You've come from Fowey,' remarked the harbour-master
at Salcombe. 'Now did you see my friend the harbour-master
there?' We hadn't seen or heard of him. 'There you are now,'
he was pleased at proving his point. 'That's because it's a
commercial port. Jim doesn't bother his head about yachts.
But what would we do here if I didn't collect from sailing folk.
That'll be four shillings please.' But it was the harbour-master
at Dartmouth who was the most impressive. He appeared
from nowhere in his motor-boat (the engine did his bidding
like an obedient dog), immaculately uniformed and quite
appropriately silhouetted against the Victorian facade of the
Royal Naval College on the south bank.

   The town of Dartmouth has many colourful facades, bright
with wood-carving, painted scrolls and fillets, some very old,
some not-so-old copies. One inn boasts that Drake stood up at

the long bar and drank to the defeat of the Armada. In some parts the houses are built right to the water's edge with boats moored in deep water just below them. Dartmouth is an excellent port of call. It has fine scenery, deep water right up the river, ample room for mooring or anchorage and a marina into the bargain.

The next day we had to start the long haul east to Poole with no convenient ports of call en route. And the weather was getting worse. The burgee at the masthead was fluttering like a wild bird in a cage when, on a grey Wednesday afternoon at 1500 hours, we tore downstream with a full ebb tide, the sails tight, a capsized, water-logged racing-dinghy on the north shore to cheer us on our way. Outside there was a big yawl carrying a storm jib and tiny mizzen, which shortly turned and went in again to Dartmouth. The glass was falling and the weather report had given gale warnings in the Dogger Bank area with 'northerly Force 6, locally 7' in the Portland-Plymouth area. There were white caps on the waves and the wind was sounding in the rigging, though not so shrill as it was to sound by dawn. Before dark I changed to a smaller jib and rolled the mainsail down past the first batten.

Our course was 090 and I tried to point as high as I could into the north-east wind to allow for leeway. I think I sailed badly all night, pinched her too much, and lost more ground than if I had let her sail a point or two more off the wind. It was a wet, uncomfortable night with rain squalls and the sea bumping up between the floats and sloshing sideways into the cockpit. The log fouled and I couldn't clear it. But by 2130 hours we picked up the Portland Bill light and kept it steadily winking on our port hand until dawn. There was plenty of other shipping, and I fired one white mini-flare for a steamer that passed easily under our stern. The wind and sea steadily increased and as the night wore on I strained my eyes for a sight of Anvil Point Light which has a range of eighteen miles. But in vain. We were too far south and the wind seemed more east than ever. Dawn broke drearily with only a heaving waste

of water in sight and the wind howling dismally. I had to have
a rest and change into dry clothes, and thought *Sophie* might
lie more comfortably if I got the sails down and put out a
bucket as a sea-anchor to hold her bows to the wind. I tied a
bucket to ten fathoms of warp, but it was far too light. She
preferred to lie (easily enough) broadside on, lifting with each
wave, the weather float bumping down into the deeper
troughs. I took my clothes off, got shivering into a sleeping-
bag and had some tea, warming and restoring. By 0800
hours I felt fit to go on indefinitely.

We had been doing no better than 065 on the port tack, so I
got her round on to the starboard tack pointing 340 or better,
and all day we laboured north with no sight of anything but
the sea and the sky and passing steamers. By late afternoon
the steamers were passing south rather than north of us, the
wind was down to Force 4 or 5, and about 1900 hours we
sighted a long, low headland on the starboard bow. Was it
Portland Bill, Anvil Point (as we hoped) or St Catherine's
Point? In the event it turned out to be Peveril Point and the
Anvil Light came up dead ahead. We still took hours to beat up
to Poole, but with the lights of Swanage, Studland and
Sandbanks welcoming us, it was like the epilogue to a play.
We blundered around in the dark and finally anchored off
Canford Beach in ten feet of water. Next morning we moved
inside and spent Friday cleaning up the boat. It was a
beautiful spot to work in - south of the sandy beaches and
white cliffs of Brownsea Island, and encircled to the west and
south by the low, green hills of Purbeck, the rising stretches of
Wych Heath, Newton Heath and the bird sanctuary in the
Little Sea behind Studland Bay.

That was how I changed to multihulls. We had covered
some 400 miles over the water in about seventy-five hours'
sailing. It had been in all sorts of weather with a fair
proportion of light and unfavourable winds, in deep and shoal
waters, and with a minimum crew. Except when going to

windward close-hauled and reefed down (and there my reefing and trying to sail too close may have been at fault), *Sophie* had behaved like an angel, and all in all been comfortable, flexible, easily handled, safe and fast.

As a result of this cruise, I had found that my little four-tonners were not adequate for what I wanted. If there was only a light wind they were sluggish, and if the wind got up, the sea got up with it and took all the way off the boat. The accommodation spoiled the sailing qualities and yet was not enough to be really comfortable. For a monohull at that length a converted day-sailer (a Dragon boat with an awning say) with all the attendant discomfort of camping in the cockpit, might be a better bet. For monohulls it seemed that twenty-five (the Folk boat), twenty-seven or thirty feet was the minimum for a yacht that was going to make open-sea passages of more than a few miles.

Of course it was not a fair comparison to consider these boats alongside *Sophie,* a thirty-foot trimaran. But generally speaking multihulls are not so handicapped by lack of length. *Three-Fingered Jack,* a trimaran twenty-four feet on the water-line, came tenth in the 1970 Round-Britain Race. The little catamaran, *Hirondelle,* twenty-two feet overall, can hold her own in the company of much bigger boats. Because multihulls can to a certain extent plane on the water, they are not subject to the limitation of speed given by the formula

$$V/ \ L \ 1.4$$

where L is the water-line length and V the speed. Again small multihulls can offer better accommodation. In accommodation, a catamaran is almost the equivalent of two or even two-and-a-half boats of similar water-line length and a trimaran the equivalent of one-and-a-half.

I am no authority on the vexed question of monohulls and multihulls, but without saying anything new, perhaps I can summarise the points of advantage and disadvantage as I see them. No multihull can offer the ultimate stability of a keel boat which will right itself when turned upside-down. On the other hand, the risk of capsize for multihulls *can* be reduced to such an extent that it is not much more likely then being struck by lightning. As against this risk, multihulls can, and often do, carry built-in buoyancy which, unless they are very heavily laden, will render them unsinkable. This is not possible with a keel yacht, as many tragic holings and sinkings testify.

Multihulls don't heel over like monohulls which makes them more comfortable in some respects, and does away with the need to have everything held down, tied down, or in gimbals. They also dry out easily and upright without legs, and in shoal waters their lesser draft can be an advantage. On the other hand, their motion may be more agitated than that of a monohull, since they are floating on top of the water, and for this reason some people may get seasick on them more easily. Monohulls can cope with shoal waters by internal ballast and centre-boards or twin bilge keels. Multihull cabins give me a feeling of more light and space since they are more on top of the water. Sometimes even in quite big monohulls, the only daylight entering the cabin comes from overhead skylights.

The speed of multihulls has been exaggerated. To be *very* fast, multihulls have to take risks by crowding on canvas; they have to skimp on accommodation to cut down windage, and they have to reduce weight to such an extent that engines, equipment etc may have to be sacrificed. But even so, taking the case of cruising boats fully equipped and heavily laden, multihulls are substantially faster than monohulls on a reach or running. When it comes to sailing close-hauled there is not much in it. Multihulls don't go about so easily, and unless they have adequate centre-boards or fin keels, may make more leeway.

Multihulls are often at a disadvantage in manoeuvring in confined waters. They have more windage and less grip in the water. I have found that some multihulls, even under engine, will turn more strongly and quickly, especially into the wind, with the centre-board down. Again their beam is a disadvantage and an added expense in crowded anchorages and marinas, though one trimaran, the *Ocean Bird*, aims to meet this problem with moveable floats. It may be this last factor of berthing or mooring which accounts for the very slow increase in the popularity of multihulls, considering that they do have a number of positive advantages, especially in the smaller sizes. Otherwise it can be put down to the conservatism of the crowd. Multihulls as pleasure yachts have been known only for ten years, monohulls for seventy or more.

CHAPTER FOUR

AURORA BOREALIS

And brief the sun of summer in the North

- Tennyson

I hadn't owned a boat myself now for twenty years, and I began to think about buying one. I recognised the advantages of chartering - one doesn't spend nine months of the year working on maintenance and repairs, to have the boat in good trim for the remaining three months' sailing. The charterer finds everything ready for him, crams a lot into a short period, and though he pays (usually at a high rate) for wear and tear and any damage, he still hasn't got to worry about the boat when he's finished with it.

At the same time there is some magic in ownership. In these socialist days private property is often condemned. But there is ownership and ownership, and for the small, do-it-yourself sailor it can mean a greater degree of devotion, caring and appreciation. Never to bother about the maintenance and upkeep of a boat and its gear means missing a range of yachting experience and enjoyment as well. From a certain point of view the charterer and hirer are opting out of a responsibility, and paying somebody else to assume it, for everything has to be cared for, whether it is old furniture or new boats.

There is always the question of money. Multihulls are not popular with marine finance companies, and I hadn't saved anything out of income since Hong Kong days when I was a blood-sucking imperialist. However, I had been left a small legacy by an aunt in New Zealand, and if I searched the market carefully and bought second-hand. . . . .

So I looked at a lot of boats. Before I make remarks about them and provoke designers and owners to attack me, I had better say that they represent only first impressions and personal ones at that, affected perhaps by what I had for breakfast or what glasses I was wearing, as well as by the strength, speed, comfort and safety of the craft themselves. I went up to Deganwy in North Wales and spent a week-end sailing in one of James Wharram's Polynesian catamarans. We went round to the Menai Straits and the scenery of hills and peaks in Snowdonia was delightful. But I didn't find the boat (perhaps because it had loose-footed sails which I wasn't used to) so easy to handle or so good to windward. I went to Brightlingsea and sailed an Iroquois for an afternoon with Reg White. She handled beautifully but I wasn't sure. I took a train to Gourock near Glasgow and went out in a Piver Nimble. She had been well looked after and seemed in good condition. But I felt that the light construction wouldn't stand up to the bumps and scrapes a yacht has to expect in her working life.

I went up to Berwick-on-Tweed to look at a Jim Brown 40ft trimaran. I liked the centre cockpit and she looked fast and strong. But she was too expensive and I didn't think gave enough accommodation (which at the time I was rather looking for) for the money. I had a sail in a Prout Ranger from Canvey Island. She had a nice open-plan design, but seemed a bit slow in the light airs that blew that day. I tried a Cox Waverider, a neo-Piver design with a fixed keel instead of a centre-board. She sailed well but she was expensive and some features of the layout were awkward. I went to Jersey where, in a field surrounded by ruminating cows, a Rudy Choy Polycon catamaran was undergoing a refit. She was strong and undoubtedly fast, but I had to double up to get into the cabin, and I didn't think I could stand it on a long cruise. I drove down to Christchurch and went out in a Bobcat. The accommodation was good but I wanted something that would sail better. I went down to Mylor Harbour in Cornwall and looked at a way-out trimaran, designed and built by a real enthusiast, but she looked like the Ark on floats, and I went away unconvinced. At successive Boat Shows I looked systematically at all the new multihulls, but new boats like the girls draped over them, were beyond my budget.

It isn't easy to decide about boats. You can look at the layout, get a list of the equipment, and get a surveyor to examine the hull. Sometimes you can take her out for a sail. But you don't really know her. Most boats behave differently in light airs or strong winds, heavily or lightly laden, with a different trim, with different sails - and it is impossible to experience the full range of conditions on any trial, however extensive. Often in the nature of the case, a boat for sale isn't in the water and you have to take her sailing qualities on trust. On the whole, I think it is probably safest to stick to a popular production boat that has been established for at least a few years. A readiness to experiment may bring substantial rewards, but one should be prepared to cut one's losses. Some people would regard the whole of the multihull market as coming into the experimental category, but, without going into detail, there are a number of production trimarans and catamarans built for speed, accommodation, strength, safety, or a balance of these and other factors, which now have solid, established reputations, and can be relied on to fulfil what is expected of them. Many of these boats are not cheap, and I think the notion that multihulls are cheaper than monohulls needs some modification. Light construction and amateur construction are one thing, but if multihulls are to have the same strength, quality of finish and durability over the years, as is taken for granted with monohulls, then this has to be paid for.

During this time I had a last cruise in *Sophie* from Yarmouth round the coast to Maldon. It set the pattern of a later, longer voyage, a pattern of starting out in company, then continuing alone because I was stuck for somebody to go with me. Jonny had done some sailing on his own, and had been one of the crew on a cruise from the Medway to Tynemouth, which ended disastrously when they got caught in a gale, tried to get assistance from a larger vessel and damaged the mast in the process. However, undeterred, he joined me at Yarmouth in the Isle of Wight, and we set out on a Thursday morning, west through the Solent with a fair tide but a wind from the east. I was under the weather having eaten some bad oysters the night before, but while I steadily got better, Jonny steadily got worse. We spent the night in Chichester Harbour, off Hayling Island, then set sail on Friday with a north-easter which took us roaring down to Selsey Bill, but caught us slap on the nose together with a nasty, short chop, as soon as we rounded the point. As we beat up towards Brighton, Jonny got sicker and sicker.

'Do all multihulls bounce up and down like this?' he asked crossly. However, he wouldn't give up and go below, but stayed on deck to help with tacking and sail changing. Finally when we got in under the cliffs west of Newhaven, it was 1700 hours and Jonny was worn out, so we motored the rest of the way into Newhaven Harbour to a rather dusty berth alongside a trawler on the east side of the port.

Seasickness is a funny thing. On a monohull Jonny isn't a bad sailor, but the motion of the trimaran laid him low. Camilla came out to cook for us one week-end and found that she could stand anything except being in the galley. I remember a visit to one of the outlying Seychelles islands when we went there on a slow boat and came back on a very fast one. There was a couple on board who did the trip both ways. Going there on the slow boat the wife was sick and the husband, who felt fine, made some jokes at her expense. But coming back on the fast boat the tables were turned. She felt fine while he was sick as a dog. I usually slip fairly easily into the boat's motion and get my sea legs without even a single pill. But sometimes something goes wrong (one cruise it was trying to do last-minute carpentry with my head down) and I get violently ill. The malady may take different forms and, as

as the usual nausea and vomiting, I have experienced
gestion, constipation, headaches, cold fits, insomnia - all
as forms of seasickness. Different remedies seem to suit
different people, so one should have a selection on board.
Non-medical remedies are often effective: fresh air and something to do - and of course time. Three days at sea in a small
boat, and most people will have forgotten that seasickness ever
existed. But while it does it has to be recognised and taken
seriously.

Saturday was a lazy day in port. Jonny slept it off. The
family (Jane, David, Chris, Camilla) came down for tea and we
all went for a sail round the bay. I wanted to get on, the
forecast was westerly Force 4, and I proposed an overnight sail
up the coast. But nobody was keen to accompany me, and
finally I waved them goodbye at 1830 hours and outside put
her head east. I held the westerly all night - round Beachy
Head, past the Royal Sovereign at a steady six knots, along the
coast past Eastbourne and Hastings, past the Rye Marshes
(fewer lights now) to Dungeness, then in the small hours up to
Folkestone and on to Dover. Dover Harbour with blazing
flood-lights looked at 0500 hours like some strange other
world. It was the perfect night passage, and the only mishap
was losing a torch overboard. I had picked it up to look at the
compass and somehow it slipped from my grasp, went
skittering across the deck and into the sea. I tied *Sophie* up to
a visitors' mooring, slept until 1000 hours, reported at the
yacht club and got permission to leave her until the next
week-end, and about noon caught a train to Redhill.

We came back to the boat the following Thursday night.
This time for crew I had two Japanese sisters who were visiting
London. One was a film journalist, the other a musician and
they had been recommended to me for introductions and
assistance. Tony had said they might come, and he was to join
us on the Friday evening with a school-teacher friend, Roger,
after we had sailed the boat from Dover to Ramsgate. It was a
very modest passage of twenty miles and we had a whole day to

cover it. Tokiko and Masako were both good swimmers. They had been boating, they were used to other sports, and I was glad to have anyone who could pull a rope or handle a boathook. They were very keen to go sailing, and Tokiko brought a bottle of soya sauce to go with the mackerel they hoped to catch - to be eaten raw of course. In the train Masako gave a demonstration of paper folding - making dozens of objects quickly and skilfully with the most intricate patterns. Most striking was a seagull with wings high as if about to land on the water.

We got away from Dover to a good start at 1000 hours on the Friday and ran up the coast with a fresh, following breeze. I took the inner channel but found the buoys difficult to pick up, the second and third buoys seemed further to the west, further inshore, than shown on the chart. As a result we twice got into shoal water under five feet. However, that was still safely over *Sophie's* draught and we got to Ramsgate at 1300 hours (three hours for the twenty miles) and, under the engine, successfully negotiated the strong cross current at the entrace. We moved several times trying to find a comfortable berth against the heavy wooden piles of the sea-wall, finally lying outside a derelict-looking six-tonner which acted as a large fender. It was one of the occasions when a plank to lay along the side of the boat would have come in useful. We got in some provisions and wandered round Ramsgate, a neat, busy town. At the port British Ford cars were loading for Germany, while Volkswagens were being unloaded for British buyers.

Tony and Roger arrived at midnight on Friday, and we left Ramsgate at 1015 hours the next morning, bound for Burnham-on-Crouch. There were gale warnings in the Thames area, but Tony happily set sail saying they usually took the cautious view, and the worst of the weather was further north. The wind was north-west and we beat up to the North Foreland close-hauled on the port tack, then went about on the starboard tack along the Kent Coast to Whitstable and the Isle of Sheppey. Then again on the port tack, across the

Thames estuary to the Shivering Sand Forts and the Black
Deep. It was rough and cold and uncomfortable. Masako sat
in the cockpit like a carved figure, eyes closed, stoical, but
clearly feeling sick. Tokiko wouldn't eat or drink. Roger was
cheerful and chatty, then violently sick over the side. Only
Tony and I had a hearty lunch.

The day wore on with the wind persistently against us, and
though the sea eased, we didn't reach the entrance to the
Crouch until nightfall. Tony seemed a little apprehensive
about going in at night. But the wind had fallen right away
and we motored peacefully in, following the one lighted buoy
and leading marks near Southend aerodrome. Then we picked
up each subsequent buoy with a torch as we came to it. We
reached Burnham at 2230 hours, rowed ashore to meet Ann,
Richard and Anthony (who were to sail to Maldon on the
Sunday), and, after a drink at the yacht club, somehow all
eight of us turned in and slept on board.

During my search for a boat to buy, I had read in an
Amateur Yacht Research Society publication, *Catamarans
1969,* about a Swedish catamaran, *Dacapo 24,* designed by
Heinz-Jurgen Sass which sounded interesting. At the same
time there appeared in *Multihull International,* to which I was
now subscribing, a short account with photographs of a 35ft
version of this design, which had been built at Holmsund, a
timber port in the north of Sweden. It had been built by
Erland Sjöstrom, a marine engineer working at the port, his
brother Rolf, and a friend Lennart Lindborg. They wrote, 'we
have sailed about 2,200 miles . . . in winds exceeding 50 knots
and reached speeds up to 24 knots in open seas. . .'; there
were drawings of the layout and sail plan, and one of the
photos was marked: '*Pussy Cat* at eighteen knots'.

I decided to write to Sass in Stockholm, asking how many
boats had been built to this design, how they performed, what
building costs might be, and so on. I didn't really expect
anything to come of it; it was more of a fan letter, written

simply for its own sake. However, he replied, saying about five boats had been built, several in Stockholm and the largest in Holmsund. The cost of building in Stockholm (which was all he knew about) was high, somewhere in the region of £8,000 or £9,000 for a 27ft boat, which was way beyond my means.

But only a week or two later I had another letter from him. The owners of the boat built in Holmsund wanted to sell her. They had built *Pussy Cat* intending to sail her (the three of them) to the West Indies and go into the charter business. Now they were all engaged to be married to Swedish girls, and the partnership was breaking up. He gave me an address and I wrote to it. The people there sent me more particulars of the boat, another photograph in colour, and the price they wanted in Swedish krone which came to about £6,000. I took a deep breath and sent back an offer of £5,000, subject to viewing her, satisfactory condition, possible survey etc. etc. The reply came back that my offer represented only the cost of the materials and fittings that had gone into the boat, but - they would accept it.

So near the end of February 1970, I found myself pushing £70 into the middle of the roulette table in the shape of an air flight to Holmsund (accent on the *sund*) to go and view *Pussy Cat*. Having looked at so many boats without being able to make up my mind, I was sure this would be another wasted journey. I salved my conscience by arranging a couple of meetings in Stockholm (where I was also to see Sass) with film people - that at least would be business.

Sass met me at the air terminal, spent nearly a whole day showing me over the capital and in the afternoon saw me on a bus to the airport to catch a plane for Umeå, a sizeable town a few miles inland from Holmsund. Despite limited English he talked knowledgeably and at length about boats. He gave me a copy of his book, *Catamaraner och andra Flerskrovsbåter,* a short work, but full of technical details, graphs of wind resistance, speed, stability, comparison of different masts, centre-boards, sails. Unfortunately as my Swedish is confined

to words like smörgåsbord and Greta-Garbo, I could only look
at the pictures and be impressed by the graphs. Perhaps one
day it will be translated. *Pussy Cat*, he told me, had 'no
bathroom finish', by which I gathered that the mat of the
fibreglass showed on some of the surfaces. They had altered
some of the design details; in his opinion she was under-sailed,
but she was strongly built and well equipped.

In Stockholm the temperature was minus fifteen degrees
Centigrade and the sea had been frozen. But the streets had
been swept clear of snow, the air was crisp and clear and all
the buildings warmer than in England. As we flew north over
Uppsala there stretched below us dark armies of fir trees, their
bristling spears thrusting through the snow. Evening stole in,
a blue haze. The aerodromes were like fairyland - white tinged
with purple and darker blue lights, like violets to guide us in.
Then as we flew north in the gathering dark there were
glimpses of a nightmare landscape: sea and land merged in
endless chasms and twisted hills of ice and snow, grim and
forbidding and utterly desolate. A fit setting for the Norse
sagas and the violent turmoil of the Ring. Past Sundsvall,
Harnösand and Ornsköldsvik we flew until we came finally to
the lights of Umeå. Holmsund lies south of the Arctic Circle
about the same latitude as Iceland, but as the whole Gulf of
Bothnia freezes (motor-car expeditions have been made across
the frozen sea to Finland), the climate is far more severe. The
brothers met me at Umeå airport and we drove about ten
miles to Holmsund where they had booked a room at the local
hotel. Then we went to Rolf's flat for supper. We were to see
the boat the next day.

The port of Holmsund operates all the year round, export-
ing wood pulp from the surrounding pine forests. Everything
is adapted to the climate. In winter ships especially built for
the job, break a way through the ice. All the loading is under
cover, loads being moved on shore by heavy, box-frame
crane-lorries with electro-magnetic lifters and swung on board
by electro-magnetic cranes, with the drivers in both cases

inside heated cabs. Some buildings and car-parks had rows of sockets on the outside wall for plugging in car heaters. Everyone wore furs and fur hats, and cloakrooms in hotels, restaurants and houses were outsize by our standards. All about there were large scoops and bulldozers to keep roads open, and small scoops and light shovels for drives and side paths. People went shopping with little sledges, and babies were pushed by their mothers in closed in pramsledges and with a little window. Doors and windows were double or triple glazed, and the hotel was as warm as toast. There seemed to be lots of cafeteria meals and the main features of Swedish food, as I experienced it, were the number of different types of bread and biscuits and the fact that they served potatoes with everything. When I left they wanted to give me a present of strongly flavoured, locally-tinned fish. But the tins were bulging dangerously which is apparently their normal state and in the end we decided it would be too much of a risk to take them up in the plane.

We drove down to the port in the morning and found the boat in a vast warehouse on the quayside. She looked huge out of the water and the accommodation was spacious. If you could sleep eight on *Sophie* at a pinch, then you could squeeze fourteen into *Pussy Cat*. I went over everything with the greatest care as I would be unable to arrange a survey. All solid, all sound, most of it looking brand new. There was the mast made of fibreglass by Plymspar, a Swedish firm, there were massive French winches, heavy blocks, stays, chain-plates. There was an electrical Aga log, Webasto warm-air heater, Primus gas cooker, fluorescent lighting, SL 400, two anchors, chain and line. I went to somebody's house and saw the outboard motor, a Penta Archimedes U40. There was no echo-sounder, no guard rails, no spinnaker, no built-in water tanks, no dinghy, no self-steering. Still, it was the best value I had seen. I decided to buy her.

I told them this in the afternoon and they were pleased. We talked all that evening about various arrangements, as I was catching a plane back to Stockholm the next morning. They offered to help me sail *Pussy Cat* to England; they wanted to make the voyage anyway. They would repaint her for me if I let them know what colour I wanted. They would fit water tanks, Erland said, in the fin keels. Each would hold about twenty-five gallons and it would keep the weight low down. He was also planning to fit new, stronger rudders. If I sent them an echo-sounder and self-steering gear, they would fit them for me. The life-lines and spinnaker I would leave until I got her to England. I would send them a deposit, ten per cent, as soon as I got back, and make arrangements to get the rest of the money from New Zealand.

How soon would I be able to sail her back? Not until June at the earliest, they said. The thaw would come before that but the sea wouldn't be free of ice. Also it would take them until then to get the boat ready. They would provide a crew for the voyage if I could get someone to do the cooking. I caught the plane in the morning from Umeå. Back in Stockholm I kept my film appointments, but my mind was on the boat.

It seemed I had the boat I wanted, something solid enough for long cruises and big enough to live on board if I wanted to. I also had ideas about 'taking people out' and *Pussy Cat* would lend herself to this. First, however, I had to get her to England and berth her there. The worries of a boat owner cast their shadows before me as I searched the south and east coasts for a suitable mooring, finally arranging with a boat-yard at Hoo on the Medway for a tidal mud berth, but one that would be alongside. It was as near as possible to London and the cost was only ninepence (pre-decimalisation) a foot a week. Elizabeth agreed to come and do the cooking on the voyage from Holmsund, and on Saturday May 30 we got the plane from London Airport. It took us five hours flying to get to Umeå. It was to take sixteen days to sail back.

In the meantime I had been occupied getting various bits of gear and arranging to get them to the boat. I had a meeting with a Swedish sea-captain in a Chinese restaurant in Soho, which might have come out of the pages of Conrad. He was captain of one of the two or three cargo boats which ply all the year round between Holmsund and London, keeping us supplied with kitchen rolls, paper bags, table napkins and the rest. The Swedes themselves seem to go in for paper products and on the boat the boys had paper sheets and pillowcases, paper throwaway plates and cups - and perhaps a thousand pieces of throwaway plastic cutlery! Anyway the captain knew the Sjöstroms and he was prepared to take my bits and pieces of equipment. In fact he so enjoyed his Chinese meal, that he offered to take me as well, and I think he meant a free passage. It would have been an interesting experience, but I couldn't really spare the time, so I had to say no.

I had trouble, too, getting the money out of New Zealand. The Reserve Bank had to give a permit and this was delayed. However, after an exchange of urgent telegrams, I finally got one dated May 26 which read: 'Transfer despatched by cable to Swedish Landbank, Umeå account number vwxyz.' This gave a few days' margin and I thought it would be OK. Besides a large roll of charts, I also carried with me on the plane the last bit of equipment to turn up, a Champ battery charger to make up for the lack of any alternator or generator on the outboard engine with its hand-start.

It was a very different Sweden we flew over this time. Stockholm was warm and sunny, as gay, with the lightly-dressed crowds, as a Mediterranean city. The fir forests were free for a few months from their winter blanket, and the grim avalanche of snow and ice had turned into a picturesque coast line. But what was that white patch? Floating ice clear enough, and the size of a hockey-field by the look of it. In Umeå and Holmsund all the snow had gone, but both towns looked a little damp and dishevelled as if they were more used to being with snow than without it. Down on the quay *Pussy Cat* was lying alongside, smart in her new coat of paint, with water-tanks, rudders and echo-sounder fitted. We settled on board and as it was still below freezing at night, kept the Webasto warm-air heater going.

We had parties in the boys' houses, and it was strange to sit until midnight with the daylight still outside. A ghostly daylight in which the world beyond the window-pane grew eerie, and there were gnomes and goblins behind each bush. I had hoped to get away on Monday, but for one thing the money had not arrived, for another the food had still to be bought. So on Monday we ordered food for five for a fortnight, then went into the Landbank in Umeå, where the business counters were flanked with as many easy chairs and tables as a hotel lounge. There, after an anxious wait, a lot of to-ing and fro-ing in Swedish, telephone calls to Stockholm, and production of identity documents, the money was, somewhat to my surprise, counted out to me in an impressive pile of Swedish bank-notes. I then handed it to Erland. They proceeded to divide it into three piles, and we all signed the bill of sale for the Swedish authorities and the English customs. We then proceeded to lunch at the town's best hotel, a delightfully old-fashioned establishment, where we had a memorable fish course of local prawn pancakes, followed by an excellent claret with the main dish.

There was to be a last minute substitution in the crew. Lennart had fallen out, since he and his girl friend were married, and she was imminently expecting a baby. Large and cheerful, she was one of the merriest at the parties, and she went into hospital the day we sailed. Lennart's place was taken by Kjrell (pronounced Shell), a radio ham who filled the saloon with radio gear and aerials. Tuesday we did some last minute shopping, cut plastic tubing as battens for the sails (there was 120ft in the fully-battened main and mizzen), filled up with water, and finally cast off at 1600 hours on June 2.

It had been an enjoyable two days - busy with the pleasure of planning; charged with the excitement, the anticipation, the apprehension perhaps, that attends any venture however modest.

CHAPTER FIVE

SOUTHWARD BOUND

The way is long to the sun and the south

-Swinburne

A small group of families and girl friends gathered on the quay to wave us goodbye. Earlier there had been visitors on board, jokes, discussions, farewells. Erland, the senior Swede and boatbuilder, a big, strong fellow with a wry sense of humour and a little bit of a showman, took confident charge of everything. He was proud of his creation as well he might be, and he took a pride, too, in being able to handle her well. Rolf, his younger brother, followed his lead and there was a close bond between them. Once when Rolf had fallen asleep in the cockpit exhausted, I saw Erland looking down at him as tenderly as a mother might look at her child. Kjrell, smaller than the other two, was lithe, dark and energetic, with a sharp, sardonic tongue, but as I had no Swedish, much of his wit was lost on me. I was delighted to have them on board and to leave most of the sailing to them. In a way they were having a last fling, as no owner likes parting with his boat. I planned to put them up, show them round, and repay some of their hospitality when we got to London. But as it turned out I didn't get the chance.

The Swedes were important to the cruise in another way. They knew all about the boat and her gear. Furthermore they were technicians, and could cope with engines, batteries, lighting circuits and the rest, far better than I could. I could manage the sailing and navigation, but though the distance was some 1,300 miles, it was not going to be a difficult cruise from that point of view. Much of the time we would be coasting, and even if out of sight of land, we would be surrounded by radio beacons in easy range, and in some cases with buoys or light vessels far out to sea.

After casting off we moved slowly under the engine, in a flat calm, past little wooded islands, then past Bredska Lighthouse, steering approximately south by west, 197 degrees. Gradually we collected a little wind from the north-west and continued on through the cold, bright night - the northern night which is never dark, even at midnight. The sun would set at 2300 hours and rise again by 0100, but the hour or so in between was full daylight and there were no stars. I have never seen such brilliant skies, and the pinks, the crimsons, the blood-red shades that suffused all the heavens and painted the clouds, lasted for hours. There was warm colour in the sky, but on the sea it was deadly cold and even with the heater going, it was too chilly for anybody to sleep well.

All Wednesday, out of sight of land in moderate seas, we sailed south down through the Gulf of Bothnia and with variable force winds from the west making three to five knots. Our first landfall would be Fingrundet, or Finnish Rock Lighthouse, about forty miles north of the Aland Strait. We sighted the lighthouse (not the light because there was no darkness) during our second night at sea, about 0400 hours on Thursday morning, on the starboard bow. But it was to take us three more days to get through the Strait and past the islands off Stockholm. The wind which had been light but always with us from the west or north-west, died away completely, and for the best part of three days we lay becalmed in the Baltic, relieving the monotony by running the outboard motor for an hour or two every now and then. On Thursday, too, we saw floating ice and heard an ice warning on the radio.

Becalmed in the Baltic. There was brilliant sunshine practically day and night, and it was bitterly cold. Leaving out Elizabeth who had meals to contend with, we kept watch, two

at a time. I would have preferred one, and more time off, but
the Swedes wanted company, and in any case both the cold
and the light made it difficult to sleep off watch. It was tiring
but there was a magic fascination about it. For there were all
kinds of mirages - strange shapes on the horizon; green fields
in the sea; land and cities beyond the rim of the earth; and
even ships steaming upside-down in the sky. And not only the
sky, but the oily sea itself ran red and green at sunset.

With our slow progress the Swedes seemed to become
restless. I think they began to be disenchanted with the idea of
sailing to England from then on. Erland told me for the first
time that they wanted to be back in Holmsund for the
Midsummer Festival on June 21 and 22. There was talk of
calling at Marienhamm in Finland and at Visby on the island
of Gotland. We had other minor troubles. Kjrell had frequent
radio-telephone conversations with other operators in Sweden
and they seemed to take a lot out of the batteries, as did the
fan of the air heater, while the little generator I had brought
was not sufficient to recharge them. The Aga log became
fouled with seaweed and other than diving under the boat,
there was no means of clearing it. This meant we had to guess
our speed, and what was more serious for navigation, the
distance run. At the beginning of the cruise the Swedes
enjoyed a bit of a binge with some bottles of spirits added to
the duty-free whisky I had brought. Then they turned to beer
and milk, but unfortunately our supply of both these drinks
was limited, and soon exhausted.

By 1900 hours on Friday we were approaching the Svenska
Björn (Swedish Bear) lighthouse near Stockholm, still travelling
only at one or two knots. Then gradually, as Friday changed to
Saturday, the breeze freshened from the north, and steadily
increased. By 1150 hours on Saturday we were in sight of
Gotskasandon (Gotland Sands) and only about 300 miles from
Holmsund with over 1,000 miles still to go. But the wind
freshened again veering slightly east, and with it the
atmosphere changed. It was warmer in the cabins and the

ts were getting dark. The strange mirage effects had disappeared like wraiths, and the horizon was sharp and clear. On we sailed, always south, down past Gotland with the lights of Visby away to port, then on Sunday we picked up Högby and the Kapeludden (Chapel Point) light on the long, narrow island of Öland.

On Monday at 0600 hours when I came on watch, we were spanking along in a good following breeze, still running along the coast of Öland Island and only about a mile off a tiny fishing port.

'Can we go in?' asked Erland. 'Only a couple of hours to charge the batteries, and get some fresh bread and milk.' I wanted to get on, and so presumably did the Swedes, but we would all enjoy a stretch ashore and some fresh food, so I agreed. In an hour's time we had felt our way into the tiny port and tied up inside the stone walls alongside the two or three small fishing boats already there. While the Swedes roared off in a borrowed car to get the batteries charged, Elizabeth and I wandered along country roads, through spring-time, green-and-gold fields with daffodils and primroses blooming in the gardens. After about quarter of an hour we got to a small general store where we stocked up well enough by pointing to the goods we wanted. Back at the boat, I filled the water tanks, then took my bathing suit to the end of the breakwater. The sea was dark with seaweed, but seemed no colder than in England. In fact it was warmer in the water than in the fresh northerly breeze, and I splashed and swam for a good ten minutes, coming out glowing and refreshed and with a sharp appetite for lunch. The others finally returned with the batteries charged, we lunched on board and set off again at 1300 hours. Our little port did not appear on the chart, but it was just south of the Segerstadt Lighthouse, and I gathered was called Grassgard, an appropriately Swedish name for our last close look at Sweden.

The wind was now pretty well due east, and as if to make up for the past days, blew a good Force 5 or 6. With everything set we were doing an estimated ten knots, and by Tuesday evening we were through the Börnholmsgat, passing the southern tip of Sweden, and before dark, had sighted distant Danish hills north of Gedser Odde (Gedser Point). It was a rough night and we turned south to the Gedser Rev light vessel, then west through the Fehmarn Belt. There are buoys well out to sea in this area to mark a channel swept clear of mines, since so many were laid during the war, that for many years there was no certainty they had all been disposed of. However, the risks are now minimal and for a multihull drawing three feet pretty well non-existent. It was difficult sorting out the many flashing buoys and on one occasion Erland (if he had not fortunately asked me) might have taken us hazardously off course through not knowing that *occ* on the English chart meant *occulting* not *flashing*.

At 0745 hours on Wednesday we passed Markesdorfer Huk in Germany, the northern point of the Fehmarn peninsula. There were long rows of bathing huts lining the beaches and busy ferries plying north to Lolland in Demark. The wind died away completely, the sun blazed down, and at 1045 hours, with twenty-five miles still to go, we started the engine. Slowly we motored across Kiel Bay and up towards the canal entrance at Holtenau. The beaches on both sides were now black with holidaymakers, and the quays and the water crowded with craft from rubber dinghies to large liners entering and leaving. The whole of the time we were there, the canal and the canal zone were busy with a never-ending stream of shipping.

We found a mooring in a quiet, tree-lined backwater, tied up at 1630 hours, and it was delightful to relax and go ashore, as we all felt tired and scruffy and pickled in salt spray. We tried to book a room in a hotel and order five baths, but none of them would accommodate us. However, we had a grand meal ashore and slept until late on Thursday morning.

The Swedes had been talking among themselves, and that evening Erland approached me and asked whether I would be

very much put out if he and Rolf and Kjrell went back to
Sweden after we had gone through the canal. They were due to
return for the midsummer weekend on the 22nd; it would be a
week-end of parties and jollification, and they had to start
work again immediately afterwards. It was now June 10.
Even if we made good time to England, they could hardly have
a holiday there, but would have to fly back almost at once.
They would be worn out, and it would be difficult for them.
Could Elizabeth and I take *Pussy Cat* in easy stages along the
Dutch coast, or could I get a friend to come from England and
help me sail the boat back?

'Of course,' I told him. 'Of course you must go back. We
shall be perfectly all right.' And so it was agreed.

All the same it was a blow I hadn't expected. I had left the
handling of the boat very much to them. The engine had its
temperamental side, and had several times given a little
trouble. I had brought a simple self-steering gear, a horizontal
wind-vane, the QME, which had been fitted on a bumpkin on
the starboard hull. But it hadn't been tried out at all, as
everybody seemed to enjoy taking the helm and there were
plenty of hands. But I refused to worry. The Sea-fix radio
direction finder had worked well, and it was a comfort when I
tried it out in Kiel on the radio switch, to be able to get the
shipping forecast on 200 kilocycles (or kilohertz as they say
nowadays) all the way from England. It made *Pussy Cat*'s
berth on the Medway seem that much nearer. Besides, the
winches and all the sailing tackle was good and strong, and I
could certainly handle the sails all right alone.

On Thursday we charged the batteries, paid canal dues,
wrote postcards. I bought some German charts of the Dutch
coast, and Erland quite unprompted bought some more and
presented them to me. After several enquiries I got directions
to the Seemansheim, a pleasant house in a back street, and we
all trooped off there in the afternoon for hot showers. We got in
more provisions from the nearest ship chandler, Herman
Tiessen, on the quayside at Holtenau, who gave us good

service at reasonable prices, certainly much cheaper than those in Sweden. We did especially well for duty-free goods, some English equivalents being a bottle of Cinzano for 39 pence, vodka 24 pence, rum 22 pence, and a very drinkable red wine 18 pence. Petrol though at the equivalent of 22½ pence a gallon wasn't so cheap for those days, and I had to buy fourteen gallons for the canal.

In the event we didn't use it. Early on Friday morning we joined a queue of boats at the lock gates. We had been puzzling over the traffic signals which on paper seemed most complicated, but when it came to the actual thing they were easy to follow, and we tied up in the huge lock with several other boats and just behind a very beamy barge, *Christina* of Hamburg. Erland, enterprising as ever, got into conversation with the bargees and arranged a tow for *Pussy Cat* for £3. It was about what it would have cost in petrol, but it would mean going faster, and with less trouble. So when the lock opened, we surged along on a long towline, hardly even needing to steer. With her twin hulls and fin keels *Pussy Cat* towed very steadily, and she proved too, unlike some multihulls, very steady at anchor. Except in Porto Cervo . . . but there is no need to anticipate that trouble until I actually come to it.

About half-an-hour from the entrance, as we were waiting at some red traffic lights, a launch came surging up from behind and ordered us by signs back to the entrance. Having cast off from the barge, we asked the reason why, to be told we hadn't paid the canal dues! We had paid the previous day (it was only about 30 Deutschmark) and had duly showed the receipt in the lock. When I waved the paper at them, they shrugged their shoulders and let us go. It had been a mistake! But by this time our plump friend, *Christina,* had gone on and we couldn't catch her. We tore along at full throttle, shouting and waving, only to see her disappear round bend after bend, steadily drawing further ahead. Then, after we had given up hope, we came upon our group of boats waiting at more red lights, slid in behind our heavy-hipped Hamburg working girl, and got the tow rope out once more.

The canal was beautiful - green banks, farms, bridges, ferries, waiting cars, towns, factories. There was bridge-building, dredging, widening the banks, a duck-shooter in the rushes, fishermen on the banks, a school picnic, a railway train - a varied, never-ending panorama of sights. And all the time we were passing ships, ships and more ships. There is a fine engraved Admiralty chart of the canal taken from a German print made in 1917, consisting of three serpentine segments fitted side-by-side into a square sheet. From beginning to end there are no locks to worry about, and we spent the rest of the day following our progress on this unusual but most elegant chart, and enjoying the scenery.

About 1615 hours we arrived at Brunsbüttel locks and cast off the tow. We had gone up a few feet in the Holtenau lock; now we went up a few feet more - so the North Sea was higher than the Baltic. Sometimes, depending on wind, weather and tides (the North Sea is tidal, the Baltic not), it would be the other way about. We had hoped to get to Cuxhaven, twenty miles down the Elbe, before dark, but outside we ran into a short, choppy head sea and a head wind. It would have been a hard beat tacking down the narrow channel, and the choppy sea made it difficult for the outboard motor. So we took shelter, motoring into the Alterhafen, a delightful little cove to the west of the locks, where we tied up among other boats just underneath an old-fashioned hotel on a grassy hill. There the Swedes made friends with a German who invited us all on board his very old but beautifully-kept motor-sailer. We sat all evening drinking in the warm, lamp-lit cabin, and it made a friendly, convivial ending to our cruise together.

CHAPTER SIX

MEDWAY OR BUST

> Down to Gehenna or up to the Throne
> He travels fastest who travels alone.
>
> *- Kipling*

Our host, who had a car ashore, offered to take Erland, Rolf and Kjrell to the airport the next day. As far as I was concerned, he suggested I would very likely be able to recruit a crew for the passage to England at the Cuxhaven Yacht Club. He also warned me about the difficult entrance to the yacht harbour and said I would need a strong engine. We didn't break up until after midnight, and after very friendly farewells the Swedes went off to the hotel with their gear, while Elizabeth and I went back to the board. For my own part I was trying hard to think soberly so as to get everything right for the passage to Cuxhaven.

We cast off at 0800 hours and motored peacefully out to find the same choppy sea and head wind. Never mind! We tacked doggedly back and forth, but when I tried to use the engine to help the sails, it faltered and petered out. Eventually about 1100 hours we got to Cuxhaven under sail alone, though it was certainly tricky going into the entrance and I was lucky to be forewarned. I tacked well beyond it, then under Genoa and half-hoisted mizzen came in, the current sweeping us back but the wind strong on the beam. We just made it nicely, sweeping into the entrance between high wooden walls, then swinging round into the yacht harbour on the port hand and coming up alongside the only vacant berth as I let the sails tumble down and rushed to hold the boat against the quay. With the reduction in crew *Pussy Cat* seemed suddenly to have grown in size, and it was quite a contrast handling her with two as opposed to five.

I had thought things out since I talked to Erland in Holtenau. I had had enough experience of coastal cruising to be sure that it would be easier to take *Pussy Cat* straight across the North Sea than down the Dutch Coast. And there was nobody I could expect to come across from England and help me. If Elizabeth wanted to come well and good. However, partly because of the repeated warnings of the Swedes saying: 'You mustn't try to cross the North Sea alone', but also I suspect because she was tired of cooking large meals for four hungry men under difficult conditions, she had got cold feet, and decided, if she could, to go back by ferry. It was a Saturday, and a half-holiday, so we rushed ashore leaving the boat tied up. I hadn't shaved or had time to change from dirty working clothes, and looked like a scarecrow. But it was worth it, for after walking miles and asking endless directions in halting German, we found a travel agency only a few minutes before they closed, who booked Elizabeth to leave on Sunday afternoon on a ferry from Bremerhaven to Harwich. The fare seemed reasonable, under £10, and she would be in London on Monday morning.

Then we hurried back to *Pussy Cat* and I reported to the harbour-master and to the yacht club, and asked if there was anyone who would like to come to England on a small yacht, also offering to pay the fare back, which I thought might be an added attraction. Sure enough when I called in an hour later, the secretary said he had found me a *mitsegler,* a young woman with a 'sailing certificate' who would come and see me. She turned up during the afternoon, pretty as a picture with golden hair and a radiant smile, but dressed practically enough in jeans and a jumper. She hadn't been distance cruising but much short sailing (her English wasn't bad) and she had *eine freundin* in London. I showed her enthusiastically over *Pussy Cat* and explained I could practically handle the boat by myself, but needed somebody to take the helm and let me sleep for an hour or two, and handle a boat-hook when we came into port. She could have half the boat to herself and no night watches. It seemed as though I had a crew, until I asked her age, and was told it was fifteen! I must have looked doubtful, for she assured me she wanted to come and would just go home, tell her parents, collect her sailing clothes and bring the famous sailing certificate. She didn't of course come back and I suppose if she had I couldn't have taken her. I decided I would have to go alone. At least, during the afternoon, I was able by cleaning the plugs and drying the leads, to get the outboard motor going again. Also the forecast was favourable with northerly winds Force 4 while the barometer which had been consistently high since our departure still stood at 1020.

We had supper in the yacht club, built on piles on the river side of the yacht basin, right at a deep bend in the Elbe. All the ships to and from Hamburg pass within a few yards, and as they came by every few minutes, it seemed as if we could have reached out and touched them. I turned in early, ready for Sunday, and got away with the tide at 0815 hours, leaving Elizabeth waving on the quay.

The first leg was a beat north-west to the mouth of the river for about eighteen miles. I started out under the motor, but the conditions were the same as the day before, a nasty, short, bumpy sea caused by the shallow water and the wind against the tide. The motor was zooming and choking. Then suddenly I noticed a sodden mass of cardboard caught round it. Instead of stopping the engine or going into neutral, I climbed down like a blinking idiot and tried to clear it by hand with the engine going. I was lucky - instead of taking my hand off, the propeller only bruised and cut one finger to the bone and another slightly. The cardboard cleared away, the engine stopped and I couldn't restart it. I bound up my bloody left hand, decided I couldn't face going back to Cuxhaven to have it seen to, and carried on under sail alone.

This spell of short tacking out of the Elbe was the hardest

part of the passage, and I was lucky it came when I was fresh. Even with big winches the jib sheets were heavy and slow to handle. *Pussy Cat*, never very good in stays, was particularly bad in such a bumpy sea, and the channel was so busy with fast shipping that any zig-zag course, especially one as slow as mine, was hazardous. Several times I missed going about. Once a big steamer hooted furiously at me - whether he was turning to starboard because of me or not I don't know but I was too busy to bother about it. An important looking, if improbable, figure in green trimmed with gold braid and with a telescope under his arm, waved me away from his light-vessel - I think it was *ELBE NO 2* - because he thought I was tacking too close. As I came near the north side of the channel I passed several enormous wrecks standing in the mud like the skeletons of prehistoric monsters, a reminder for the unwary of what can come from holding the inshore tack too long.

So I struggled on. If the tide hadn't been with me I might be there still, and as it was I didn't get clear of shoal water until 1330 hours when I got a good leg to the north, then went about on the starboard tack on course to the west and mercifully away from the shipping. I backed the jib for lunch, recharged the batteries for twenty-five minutes and rebandaged my hand. Then steering 257 degrees with the wind now free on the starboard side, I experimented with the self-steering vane and rather to my surprise, got it working. I was delighted at this release from the tiller; I was pleased to be out of the Elbe; I was content to be alone. For the first time on the cruise the boat really seemed to belong to me.

All night I sailed, then lost the wind and slept an hour at dawn on Monday. At 0640 hours I passed a buoy seventy miles from Cuxhaven. Not very good progress for the first twenty-three hours. There was no wind until noon, then light rain came with a breeze from the north which held all afternoon and evening. I passed many ships, but now in the open sea there was plenty of room. There was a French yacht, there were coasters and many German trawlers, picturesque looking craft with their little triangular mizzen sails, presumably just for steadying the boat. Though I was too far out to see them, I was by now passing the Frisian Islands, the scene of that exciting sailing spy story *The Riddle of the Sands.*

Again on Tuesday morning the wind fell light and my progress past the Terschelling Lightship seemed agonisingly slow. This corner of Holland is like the Exeter by-pass in the amount of traffic it seems to draw together at one point. I had been dozing off, when there was nothing in sight, and it would have been bliss to heave to for an hour's sleep. But with thirty ships all round me, I thought I had better keep awake. However, after I had passed this busy corner, set a course for England and was alone once more, I dropped off, still under way, though moving quite slowly through the water and relying on the self-steering.

I had only slept for half-an-hour when I was awakened by the wind freshening from the north-east, almost dead astern. Alas, I found that with the wind astern, I couldn't get the self-steering gear to control her. It might have improved matters if I had lowered the mizzen to bring the pull of the sails further forward, or better still devised some kind of twin-running rig. But I had only one genoa jib, no spinnaker, and in any case wasn't in a position to experiment with the sails. So I was stuck at the tiller pretty well from 1430 hours on Tuesday until the end of the voyage, except for short sleeps from 0300 to 0510 hours on Wednesday morning and from 0030 to 0245 hours on Thursday morning, when I stopped sailing and hove to.

The north-easter, with gradually more east in it, grew steadily stronger until at times it reached Force 6 by my hand wind-guage. My helmsmanship began to deteriorate, especially in the dark hours, and with the wind astern I gybed a good many times. It was due to a combination: of weariness because of lack of sleep, failure of concentration, and also trying to do other things as well as steer the boat - look at a chart, snatch a bite to eat or drink, check radio beacons.

Additionally there was the fact that the ketch rig wasn't ideal for running. Fortunately the gear stood up to all the strains imposed on it, but the very fact of gybing was upsetting and made for further fatigue. It became something of an obsession and though I tried the port instead of the starboard tack, the course I thought should be steered still seemed to have the boat running by the lee. Ironically, when I hove to about 1350 hours on Wednesday after twenty-four hours of running, mostly on the starboard tack, and got a really careful radio fix on three light vessels - Goree, North Hinder and Gabbard - I found I was south of my course and could have run off the wind more than I had.

At any rate, now that I had got my position, I could run for the Outer Gabbard, with the wind, still strong on the quarter, then, turning south, take one of the inner channels down to the Medway. At 2100 hours on Wednesday night I saw a flashing light ahead. The North Sea chart I was working from didn't give the flashes, and I couldn't leave the tiller to look up *Reed's Almanac* which was in the cabin, but a strong radio signal on the Sea-fix which was to hand, identified it as the Outer Gabbard. I had arrived!

I passed the Outer Gabbard and set a course for the Sunk light vessel, but the night was pitch dark and I began seeing things. I was operating on a large-scale chart by now, and I could identify the flashes of the Sunk ahead, but I had the feeling I was sailing up a hill, then into a hollow. Then again it was as if I was sailing through a forest and under great, rustling trees. I seemed to be getting closer and closer to the light vessel and all round it there seemed to be ships' lights - coasters, I thought, waiting for dawn to go in. In the dark *Pussy Cat* seemed to be surging forward faster and faster and faster. I knew however that I was well out to sea and that lights at night seem closer than they are. Nevertheless I could not get rid of the feeling that I might get too close and hit something or get into difficulties. My illusions grew stronger and stronger until in the end I got so worried about going on any longer that I hove to and went to sleep.

There are always sounds at sea - the waves, the boat, the wind in the rigging. And though thunder close at hand or the dismal howling of a storm can be disturbing enough, they are on the whole quiet, friendly sounds. They don't seem to bite into one's ears like the roar of traffic, the clatter of factories, the hammering of pneumatic drills. Mostly, if one is sailing in company, they are a natural background to the conversation. But on this passage and alone for days, I was far more conscious of them and of how like they often are to human speech. I didn't actually hear voices. The sounds were more like a sigh, a breath, a half word - as if somebody were just *about* to speak. Oh! Hi! Say! Aah! The wind in the rigging, a wave against the side, a creaking of the ship. I also had the feeling several times that there *was* somebody else on board, out of sight, in the cabin, someone I could talk to and discuss things with, the sort of feeling one sometimes has in an empty house. At the same time I knew I was alone and had curiously mixed feelings about it. On the one hand I enjoyed the complete freedom of choice it gave, on the other hand I missed being able to share the voyage with another person. I suppose I talked to myself. speculating on course, sails, weather, progress. I certainly meditated (I had joined a school of meditation some years before) sometimes aloud, saying a mantra to the sky and the sea, and the comfort and strength it gave surely helped me along.

I awoke before dawn after about two-and-a-half hours' sleep, and to my concern there was no sign of the light vessel. What I could see was the much bigger beam of a lighthouse to the north-west, flashing every five seconds. Before I could work out what it could be, it faded in the daylight. The next mark I picked up by the simple process of reading its name was the South-West Bawdsey buoy. On the chart, this put me further north than I had expected. It was clear I had been a good distance from the Sunk light vessel the previous night, hove to I had made some progress crab-wise to the north, and the big light had been Orford Ness. The wind was more east and still a good fresh breeze which came on the port beam, as I turned firmly south with still another forty miles to go. It was bright and sunny and I could hardly have had better weather for the last day's sailing. I bowled along clutching the tiller, nodding off every few minutes. Past mark after mark down Barrow Deep I went - the Rough, the North-East Gunfleet, Sunk Head. Past the Barrow Deep light vessel, the Barrow buoys numbers six, seven and eight, the Mid-Barrow light vessel, finally buoy number seventeen, and I was in the Thames. These channels give one the sweep of the open sea and yet if the weather is not too heavy, it is like sailing in a lake for they are protected by the sandbanks from the ocean swell.

Once in the Thames I steered west, then south again for the landmark of Sheerness. I passed the green wreck buoys to the west of the Medway channel, where it is said a sunken American war-time ship lies, still with many tons of explosives in her holds. Just before Sheerness I lowered the mainsail and, under jib and mizzen, prepared to go into one of the basins formerly used by the navy, where I hoped to find a berth. I had missed the tide by about an hour, and now I misjudged the strength of the tide coming out of the entrance against me. I didn't have enough way on, I lost the wind under the high stone walls, and I was carried slowly down on to a ligher tied up just outside the entrance. The men on board jumped to help me, took lines and warped *Pussy Cat* into the dock by hand. As they did so they got shouted permission from the harbour-master for me to lie alongside. I must have looked dirty and unkempt and now I had arrived I was dog-tired and fell into the water during the proceedings. By 1400 hours on Thursday I was tied up. I had covered some 320 miles from Cuxhaven in four days and six hours, and perhaps 1,400 from Holmsund in just under sixteen days, including nearly two days in port. Not spectacular, but not bad considering how long we had been becalmed.

I invited my helpers on board for a tot of rum, turned in and slept until nine o'clock in the evening, then went ashore and rang up my family and friends.

Holmsund to the Medway. Close-hauled on the port tack

Sunset from the Poole Harbour mooring

CHAPTER SEVEN

SHORT CIRCUITS : FRANCE

The best thing I know between France and England is — the sea.

-D. W. Jerrold

The next day, Friday, I rang up the boat-yard at Hoo where I
had arranged to berth *Pussy Cat*. Then I cleared customs,
loafed about and cleaned up the boat. On Saturday morning
two men from the boat-yard arrived by car. They worked on
the outboard and got it going, then one of them came on board
and we took *Pussy Cat* with the tide up the Medway to Hoo, a
few miles below Rochester on the west bank of the river. There
she was tied up next to a Dutch botter, a boat with enormous
timbers, in no condition to go to sea but solid enough to serve
as a house-boat for some time to come. *Pussy Cat* settled down
in the mud alongside her comfortably enough. This was to be
her home for the next nine months.

I now set about arranging for various jobs to be done, but
nothing happened very quickly. I didn't very much like being
at sea without stanchions and life lines, and that was one of
the first things I ordered and had fitted by the boat-yard. The
outboard engine had a hand start and one I found particularly
difficult, not being as beefy as the Swedes. When it was
lowered into the water ready for use sliding down a bracket on
the stern, the top of the engine was well below the top of the
transom. There was a single pulley fitted on the transom
opposite the flywheel which led the starter-cord up vertically.
However, half leaning over the side I could get neither power,
nor purchase, nor persistence into a vertical pull, with the
result that it was practically impossible for me to start the

engine at all. I planned to get a second pulley fitted on the top of the transom so the starter cord could be brought horizontal again, but there was some delay about this. In the meantime, late one Sunday about three miles from home, I found myself unable to start the engine. I had asked one of the mechanics in the yard about starting the engine at deck level then lowering it into the water.

'Should be all right,' he said. 'She won't overheat if you only run her for a few minutes.' So I tried it. But disastrously the engine, stuck in its bracket, couldn't be lowered, and over-heated. It meant a big repair job - new cylinder head, rings, gasket, etc. Fortunately all the parts could be obtained from London, the yard would fit them, and I was told it would virtually mean a new engine. But it was the start of a series of troubles which culminated in my having to buy two new motors, and in the end put me off large outboards as yacht auxiliaries.

While I was getting these and other jobs done, I was also thinking how best to use the boat for charter on a basis which would help cover my costs. I decided to arrange a series of cruises on which I would go as owner and skipper, taking as crew anybody who wanted to come, who would help sail the boat, and was prepared to share expenses. The question of arrangements between owner and crew is one which affects a good few people who go sailing. If it is a matter of friendly hospitality, or family outings, or a couple sailing together - then everybody is a law unto themselves. But when it is a friendly business arrangement, there seem to be three possibilities. On the one hand there is the rich owner with a paid crew, sometimes professional, sometimes amateur, sometimes a mixture. There may be a holiday element for the crew, the owner may do some of the work, but essentially they are working for him and he will provide boat, food, perhaps uniform, wages, and if necessary, outward or return fares. Then on the other hand there is the professional boat-charterer, an individual or company, taking holidaymakers out sailing, and charging enough to cover the cost of the boat, fuel, food, his own services, and make a good profit as well. In this case the crew may do a good deal of the work, keep watches, cook and so on, but they will do so on a voluntary or learning basis and only as much as they please - for in this case fundamentally, he is working for them.

I was aiming at a third arrangement in which the costs of the cruise would be shared equally among all the participants (including the owner of the boat). Everybody would also share the work equally, and there would be neither profit for the owner nor wages for the crew. I don't say I succeeded, but I certainly learned something by experience. For, during eighteen months, I arranged, including voyages to Malta and back, eight separate cruises and took out some thirty-five people. I tried to guess at a fixed charge which would be fair in relation to the length and distance of the cruise, to cover the boat, fuel, charts, harbour dues, insurance, etc. Then I would leave one expense, food and drink, which was likely to be the most variable, to be divided equally among everybody at the end of the voyage. Of course it was all very rough and ready; for instance nobody eats or drinks the same, and there are ready workers and the others who become invisible when there are chores to be done. At the same time, any small group in such close association, quickly develops a 'public opinion' which prevents anyone from too blatantly taking advantage of others.

On the whole I think I charged more proportionately for short than for long cruises. This seemed to be acceptable as people often look at the absolute rather than the relative cost of a holiday, and it takes account of the fact that a short cruise is as much trouble to arrange as a long one. Girls I charged at a lower rate or not at all, assuming they would do more of the less nautical, everyday work of cooking and cleaning up. Some were happy to prepare quite elaborate meals and do a full share of sailing and watch keeping too. Others expected easy watches or none at all. Others again were all for taking the middle watch singlehanded, but jibbed at cooking anything more troublesome than boiled eggs.

I didn't hit on any ready-made method of arriving at a charge for the boat, and I didn't by any means recover what it cost me. But then I did spend excessively on the engine, and other outgoings were for improvements. I have thought since that a fair formula would be to charge interest on the capital cost, for the period of the voyage, divided by the number of people in the crew, allowing also for the time boats are normally laid up, and adding something for depreciation or wear and tear. Then expenses such as charts, fuel, harbour dues, attributable to a particular voyage, could be charged for or shared. Any repairs or maintenance required during the voyage I paid for, but if crew did damage or lost gear overboard, I asked them to pay and nobody complained. There was a week-ender who, in broad daylight when we were close-hauled, ran into a buoy and damaged the bow because he was trying to see if he could pass it on the weather side. There was an American student who lost a top-action-winch handle (costing £7.50) overboard, because he carelessly left it on the winch while he pulled in the slack of the sheet by hand so that it spun into the sea.

I would ask for a deposit in advance as some guarantee against crew withdrawing at the last moment, but nobody ever did. For messing, I would allow for food on the boat at the beginning and the end and would let the crew work out the division if they wanted to. Also, unless they preferred to settle on the spot, I would give them time to pay for their share after the cruise was over. I suppose I felt it gave them an opportunity to object if they felt the terms hadn't been fair or they hadn't got value for their money. On many of the cruises there were set-backs, delays and breakdowns. But I warned everyone in advance that any schedules were subject to alteration because of wind or weather, mishap or accident. In fact only four people out of thirty-five didn't settle their messing bill, and three of those were on one rather bedevilled cruise. I had recruited crew through the popular press rather than through yachting papers, so that some of them, at any rate, were expecting a package-deal bargain, rather than a deep-sea adventure. And it was on the same cruise that we were stuck in port for four out of twelve days with engine trouble.

No doubt there are other equally viable, non-profit-sharing arrangements. For instance, I know of one owner who charges so much a day plus food, or at a higher rate inclusive. Another owner charges the crew and subsequently gives the money to charity, so that he is in effect sponsoring a series of sailing charity-does for the benefit of Oxfam, Shelter, Christian Aid or what have you.

Looking back, the most rewarding thing about chartering for all and sundry, was the number of people I met and liked. I can honestly lay my hand on my heart and say there wasn't one who didn't show up to advantage and for whom at the end of the cruise I didn't feel regard and respect. I had people from every sphere, from lorry driver to computer salesman, from carpenter to stockbroker. The most tedious part of the work was the arranging. There was the advertising (I found the *Cruise Index* the easiest medium and the best so far as results were concerned), waiting for applications, accepting, rejecting, getting deposits, discussing, giving information - and often not knowing until late in the day if I would have enough or too many, and how experienced they would be.

The first cruise I arranged was in September 1970. It was intended to last a fortnight and to take us to Cherbourg and the Channel Islands. Four people applied to come: Peter and Dave who both gave technical instruction to the apprentices in a Birmingham factory; Ken, a builder from near Rochester; and Richard from an office in Farnborough. Tokiko, one of the Japanese girls who had been on Tony's boat, agreed to come and do the cooking. Two of the crew found they only had ten days, leave, and that ruled out the Channel Islands.

However, they were all dinghy sailors without cruising experience, and agreed with Pete when he said: 'I don't care where we go. I'll be happy if we get across the Channel.' So we decided to go to Dover and Boulogne and up or down the French coast.

I had hoped to start on Saturday or Sunday, but Ken couldn't join us until Sunday night or Monday morning. It was just as well. The repair on the engine had been arranged well in advance, but the yard left it until the last moment, and when they finally tried the engine out on the Saturday morning, they found the water wasn't circulating properly, because the impeller of the water-pump had been damaged. By now we were all on board except Ken and we spent Saturday ringing up various ships' chandlers and trying to get a new impeller, but without success. We decided to drive up to London   first thing on Monday to get one, and in the meantime go out for a day's sailing on the Sunday. The yard gave us a lift off the berth with a launch and we went down to the mouth of the Medway and, with a southerly wind on the beam, sailed for an hour or two up and down the Thames, successfully getting back to the berth under sail alone. Then on Monday, struggling through heavy traffic, we got up to London and back again with the precious impeller by 1045 hours. It was fitted and the engine on board by 1430 hours, but as we cast off the boat went aground. We had missed the tide! What is more the yard brought down a bill for £77 and asked for immediate payment.

The crew were by now getting understandably impatient as we had missed three days of the cruise, and it was important to get away on the next high tide, which we did at 2050 hours down the Medway in the dark against the last of the tide which was rising until 0100 hours. We went out under the engine until I happened to look over the stern and found that the water wasn't circulating. The motor didn't seem to have overheated, but we stopped it and went on under sail. Then we lost our way. We had been following the channel buoys, but

without a large-scale chart. I had a large-scale chart of the
Thames, but it stopped at the first reach of the Medway just
above Sheerness. I thought I knew the passage up the Hoo, but
somehow this time, perhaps due to the distraction of the
engine, we couldn't pick up the next buoy, and about
midnight the bow slid aground on soft mud. I was worried as it
was very near high tide, but within minutes we were able to
carry an anchor astern with the dinghy and pull her off. There
seemed to be shallow water all round us so we dropped anchor
in thirteen feet and waited for daylight. At daylight we found
ourselves aground inthe centre of a little basin at the edge of
the main channel, having turned east towards Sheerness too
soon, and having entered the basin by the deepest part, no
more than a few feet wide.

The rest of the cruise which had started so badly was more
successful. We got away from our muddy basin about 1100
hours, and light airs took us slowly down river past Whitstable
and Margate. Peter had taken charge of the engine and found
the water would not circulate, but most ingeniously he rigged
up a substitute. He got hold of a large plastic bilge-pump and
joined a rubber tube from the outlet of the bilge-pump to a
water inlet at the top of the engine water-jacket, substituting
the rubber tube for a metal tube that came up from the
non-functioning water-pump. Then we tried the engine out
with the bilge-pump in a bucket of water, and one of the crew
steadily pumping. It worked like a charm. After half-an-
hour's running you could safely put your hand on the engine.
If anything it was probably running too cold. I will always
think warmly of Peter, not only for his enthusiastic love of
sailing, but his inventiveness and skill in improvisation.

About midnight the wind came with rain from the north-
east and increased steadily to Force 6. By dawn, after a wet
night, we were down to the South Goodwins and the wind had
backed to the west. We beat into Dover arriving in the late
morning and stayed the rest of the day there. I spent the night
on watch because of the weather. Tokiko, who had turned in,

came up cheerfully in the morning saying she hadn't slept a
wink. (I don't know anyone else who would have been so
cheerful about it.)

'It was like Tom and Jerry,' she elaborated. 'Lifting up in
the air. Bump, bump, bump.'

That was the first time I realised that *Pussy Cat* pounded
badly when beating to windward in a short sea. In the daytime
no one was much affected, but on a rough night passage it was
impossible for anyone to sleep in the centre bunks. Fortunately there were four bunks in the hulls, and on the longer
cruises I always took a smaller crew in any case. The fault was
in the construction, for the sole of the cabins between the hulls
could very well have been raised a good foot or more without
affecting the strength of the boat or the room over the bunks.
It is very much a point to watch both in catamarans and
trimarans. One sure way of eliminating it, is to design the boat
so that there is only netting, or webbing, or girders between
the hulls, but there is inevitably a loss of accommodation.
Prouts, the boatbuilders, in their latest *Snow Goose* 'tri-cat',
claim to have eliminated slamming by adding a central
V-shaped nacelle between the two hulls which breaks up the
waves. Whatever may be the result in a short head sea, it will
at any rate facilitate the fitting of a central inboard (or
inboard-outboard) engine.

Next morning, Thursday, the wind was southerly Force 5 or
6, and instead of beating south to Boulogne or Le Havre, we
decided to take the easy reach to Calais. We berthed in Calais
in good time after lunch, had hot showers in the yacht club
and a table d'hôte meal ashore of moules, tripes á la mode de
Caen and tarte aux pommes. The next day we swam - there
was a fine beach leading to very cold water - and for supper
had a French chicken and French wine on board. I have
usually been too busy going on somewhere else to realise that
Calais was anything more than a customs office and a railway
junction. But on this trip we could appreciate it as a bright,
modern town with good yachting facilities and with plenty of

shops where if the meat was dear, the wine and the fish were very reasonable. There were fine gardens and squares, the most striking monument (and what a powerful work!) being Rodin's statue, The Burgers of Calais.

On Saturday, in the absence of wind, we left for Boulogne under the motor. Ken, who had come on board laden with fishing gear and put up with some good-natured ribbing, now proved his skill catching ten mackerel and a large bass. With a dip before the meal to whet our appetites, they gave us a delicious fish lunch. We were now off Cap Gris Nez and the tide which had been helping us began to run north. Round the Cape it ran stronger and stronger until we could only just hold our own with the engine full out. Pete sensibly suggested anchoring, and though we were in fifteen fathoms of water, we managed to put together forty fathoms of line which held us comfortably. We lay there, the water racing past like a mill-stream, until slack water at 1730 hours. Then, still without any wind, we motored the last few miles along the coast to Boulogne and tied up in a forest of yachts. There was not much doing in Boulogne, with everything shut on Sunday, and nobody but me was interested in French cinema. So about noon we got under way again with a light breeze. However, no sooner did we get outside the outer harbour than an impenetrable fog blanket came down. We could hardly see from one end of the boat to the other, and we hoisted the radar reflector as high as we could get it - to the top of the main-mast. Fog horns were blaring all round us, and we kept our own going. At one point a huge shape like the side of a dim, cloudy cliff came within fifteen or twenty feet of us - then slid off agian into the mist. Somehow we struggled north and out of the fog. The tide drifted us up to Cap Gris Nez. We decided to motor to Calais before it turned, and got there at 1830 hours in time for an evening in port with French roast beef and red wine for supper.

On Monday it was time to start back. A light north-easterly started us off about noon. But outside the wind freshened, and by the time we reached the North Goodwins it had veered to the east. Rather than call at Ramsgate, we decided to make the best of the wind and press on to Hoo. We ran in past the North Foreland and up the Princes Channel, carefully picking out the lighted buoys and gradually reducing sail - first the mizzen, then the Genoa until we were running (quite fast enough it seemed in the dark) under main alone. We crossed the main channel south to the Medway buoy about midnight, then in past Sheerness. About 0100 hours, going up the Medway with nothing on our minds except determination to follow the channel properly this time, we were hailed by a customs launch. They came alongside and asked us brusquely: 'Were we from abroad?' and 'Where had we intended clearing customs?' Then they came on board, stamped our passports, and as we were all within the allowable quantities of liquor and tobacco, grudgingly gave us pratique.

No doubt cruising men should take a proper British pride in the sturdy efficiency of the British customs compared with the dreadful sloppiness of the French, who generally leave yachts-men alone or wait for them to call at the Customs House. But perhaps the less public spirited may sometimes wish our lot would ease their stern professional manner when dealing with the innocent if irritating holidaymaker, and reserve it for the serious smuggler. At any rate we escaped fines and incar-ceration and about 0200 hours got up to Hoo where we anchored outside the entrance to Hoo creek. The next day we were up at 0600 hours to catch the tide, but first the engine refused to start then the gear coupling broke. So we ended the cruise as we had begun it with engine trouble, and found our way back alongside under sail.

Over the winter I determined to get the engine properly repaired, and took it up to the agents in London. The trouble with the water circulation, it transpired, was that the lid of the water-pump had been put on upside-down. This must have occurred in the flurry of repairing the pump before we got

away, but though the yard had delayed the job then rushed it
at the last minute, it was difficult to blame them for this
specific error, since they *had* complained that there was no
workshop manual or exploded diagrams available, and it does
not seem very good design to have a lid which *can* be put on
the wrong way. I got the engine back in January and took it
down to the boat when the whole of Kent was under snow, and
Pussy Cat had full four inches all over the deck and in the
cockpit. It was cold enough outside, but I must say she looked
quite striking and most beautiful in this winter dress. The
weather was too bad to fit or run the engine, but I stayed on
board cleaning up and doing odd jobs, and with an oil-stove
going in the cabin, have never been warmer or snugger than I
was that week-end.

CHAPTER EIGHT

SHORT CIRCUITS : BELGIUM, HOLLAND, SOUTH COAST

> ... those national repugnances do not touch me, nor
> do I behold with prejudice the French, Italian,
> Spaniard or Dutch... All places, all airs
> make unto me one country; I am in England
> everywhere, and under any meridian.
>
> *- Thomas Browne*

I had arranged *Pussy Cat*'s next cruise for the end of March. The yard didn't have a free cradle suitable for hauling *Pussy Cat* out, but they were going to float her on to the concrete slipway at high tide and give me a few days (originally a week) to scrub and paint between the tides. The first effort to get her on the slipway failed for lack of water, then the next day, when there was more rise and fall, they could only leave her on for twenty-four hours from noon to noon. Fortunately, a winter in the mud seemed to have left the bottom relatively clean, except for some mud stains which nothing I could do would remove. By dark I had scrubbed the two hulls ready for painting, and the next day, starting at dawn, I got two coats on with a bit of help towards the end, just as the water came creeping in. Back in her berth, I refurbished the name on the bows in gold-transfer lettering, put some non-slip, plastic paint on the deck (I found later that it got very dirty and was difficult to clean) and cut a new set of wooden battens for the mainsail and mizzen. I was having intermittent trouble with the WC which never failed to pump out but was very temperamental about pumping in, perhaps because it had been installed too high above the water-line. The electric circuit too had been badly designed and not very well installed. The batteries were in a cockpit locker, not well enough away from weather and wet, while the fuse-board was virtually inaccessible and in a spot where a slight deck leak was causing damp and corrosion. Also, in the middle of March and barely ten days before our projected cruise, it was still snowing, and I wondered if I wasn't trying to do too much too soon.

Still a good night's sleep or even an hour spent listening to Bach's music, will work wonders, and somehow I coped with everything and got charts for Holland and some of the inland seas. The weather even improved and by Friday March 26, *Pussy Cat* was ready for a new crew and a fresh voyage. This time there were six of us - Susan, Jenny, Jack, Tony and Bill. Susan, in charge of the galley, was office secretary to a friend of mine, nautically inclined and at that time living afloat on a converted torpedo-boat on the Thames. Jenny was another office girl who had been dinghy sailing every week-end for the past three years and now wanted to go cruising. Tony was an adventurous type who had been a lumberjack and a gang worker in Canada and was currently driving a taxi in Manchester. Jack was a carpenter, despite a slight stutter an entertaining talker, a bird-watcher and a radical in politics. The nearest he had got to the water so far was in a bath-tub. He referred, perhaps slightly for effect, to *Pussy Cat*'s bow and stern as 'the front end' and 'the back end'. He turned up in a rather thin town suit and a raincoat, but given a warm coat, sailing clothes, a life-jacket and shown what to do, he took a turn at the helm and a watch at night with the rest of us. Then there was Bill, an American student who had done some sailing in the States. He was keen and more experienced, but unfortunately short-sighted and accident prone. He left a warp on the quay when we cast off, bent the pulpit rail by putting the anchor rope over rather than under it, broke the saloon table, set the Tilly lamp on fire (or was that Jack?), lost a winch handle overboard and let a halyard go up the mast (or was that Tony?)

Some of the crew were again limited for time, and we decided to confine our cruise to Belgium and Southern Holland, not trying to get to Amsterdam and the Iselmeer. Ostend was eighty miles from the Medway and this was our first objective. We left Hoo at 1330 hours with a nor'wester about Force 4, passed Sheerness at 1545 hours with the wind veering north, then the East Redsand Buoy at 1740 hours with the wind north-east and dying away. We kept going all night and sighted the Sandiette light vessel before dawn. However, our progress was slow and it was not until 1100 hours that we passed the West Hinder lightship to the north and not until 1730 hours that we picked up a buoy to the north-west of Ostend. By then the wind was due east, and we had to tack in towards the shore and lost ground with an adverse current. We didn't finally reach the Ostend entrance until 2200 hours. The engine then decided it didn't like Belgium and refused to start. We tried to tack into the harbour but the breeze was light and dead against us, funnelled by the high harbour walls, while the tide pushed us gently but firmly back. The wind was light and offshore so we anchored comfortably south-west of the entrance at one end of a bathing beach.

In the morning, after all our efforts failed to persuade the engine to work, two of us motored into harbour in the dinghy and asked for a tow, but without success. Then we returned to *Pussy Cat* and started to devise some means of towing her in, using the rubber dinghy and the little Seagull Featherweight outboard. But just at this point a small fishing-boat came out of the harbour, took a line, then once we were inside the first yacht basin, which was practically empty, cast us off and disappeared. We were in the Montgomery Dock, a very dirty basin, with the town on one side and the North-Sea Yacht Club with bar and billiard-table on the other. For lunch we had delicious fresh bread, paté, cheese and wine. Then I went straight ashore to ask about a mechanic as it was useless to consider going through any canals without an engine. I was promised one would come down to the boat early on Tuesday morning. In the meantime the crew repaired to the bar and billiard-room, which was to become their home from home for the next four increasingly frustrating days.

On Tuesday the mechanic took the engine ashore, found that the electric system was faulty and passed it on to another garage to a man he said was 'l'electricien le plus expert de la ville'. On Wednesday this expert found that one of the coils had gone and telephoned Antwerp to arrange for two new coils and a set of contacts to arrive on Thursday morning. We haunted the post-office on Thursday but the parts finally arrived by rail. They were fitted within an hour, the engine tested and brought back on board. Then when we were trying it out (Tony being a taxi-driver was Honorary Chief Engineer) the gear linkage snapped. We got the engine into forward gear and there the stubborn brute stuck - no neutral, no reverse. Ostend is a delightful town in some ways, full of rich Belgian food shops, but nobody was going to face another four days waiting for repairs, and we decided to leave on Friday morning. After all, an engine in forward gear will go through the canals, and a boat carefully handled will loose its way before hitting anything. We had a large crew quite capable of fending off in the locks or when coming alongside landing-stages.

We left Ostend at 0515 hours for Flushing with an easterly wind, tacking up the coast past Blankenberg and Zebrugge. Once in the mouth of the Schelde, the wind backed to the north and we made good progress up to Flushing (Vlissingen to the misguided Dutch), arriving there by 1430 hours. Feeling our way and following other boats, we went into an outer harbour, round a corner, then into a very big lock which took us and the other craft up what must have been six to twelve feet. Then round several more bends, we found a mooring in a snug yacht harbour with grassy banks and little wooden jetties running between the boats. The town turned out to be miles away, and as often seems to be the case when one is a visiting yachtsman, public transport was infrequent and taxis expensive.

We had decided to go on through the Middleburg Canal which ran from Flushing about ten miles northward and led eventually to the Veersemeer, a new artificial lake created as part of the Delta Plan. I wanted to allow at least six hours' daylight for the passage so as to be sure of arriving before dark, and asked everyone to be on board by 1300 hours on Saturday. But due to transport difficulties, or 'souvenir-itis' or pub-crawling, Bill and I were alone on board until 1600 hours. However, we got away pretty sharply at 1615 hours and the crew were on their toes as we manoeuvred through four bridges, each of which kept us circling until several boats were ready to pass. The town of Middleburg looked bright and bustling as we motored clear through the business centre. There was a chilly north wind against us all the way, and it began to get dark as we reached the end of the canal and the lock which was to take us a foot or so down into the Veersemeer. The lock seemed closed, another boat was tied up alongside the bank, and we thought we would have to stay there for the night. However, when I walked up to the lock-keeper's office and asked, they made no difficulty about opening for us. Veere, the town we were making for, was just round the corner and we went in slowly in the dark. But it turned out to be a tiny, crowded harbour blocked at the end by a bridge, and with no engine control, no room to turn, a following wind and not knowing in the dark exactly where to find a vacant berth, it wasn't easy. However, with some cross-talk, the help of many hands and a few light bumps, we managed and tied up alongside a quay.

Next morning was like waking up in a Vermeer townscape. Veere is the show town of this part of Holland, full of beautiful old buildings, a fantastic clock on the high town hall, a windmill over the hill. As it was Sunday morning, the streets were full of sober citizens dressed in old Dutch costumes,

black bombazine, broadcloth, lace, bonnets and buckled
shoes, solemnly walking to church with prayer books in their
hands. We stayed there all Sunday, waiting to get our
gas bottles refilled on the Monday morning. In the afternoon I
walked to the windmill. It was deserted though in good repair,
and I was able to climb by stairs and ladders up five stories,
past the huge grinders, past the cogs and spindles which join
the wind vanes to the millstones. From the top through tiny
windows, there was a view over all the country round. I went
on to the Veersemeer with my bathing-costume, but there was
something dead and unpleasant about it. There were piles of
dead wrack and seaweed at the edge and foamy scum floating
in the discoloured water. Whether it was because it had
recently been changed from salt to fresh, or whether it was
polluted by industry, I don't know. We spent the evening
playing bagatelle in the local pub and drinking the Dutch
beer, and Susan produced the most delicious fruit loaf stuffed
with every imaginable kind of dried fruit and fragrant spices.

I took the gas bottles in the next morning and got them filled
from an enormous steel cylinder. Then we set off to motor
down the Veersemeer. It was a misty morning, but we had
obtained a little coloured chart of the lake from the Veere
Yacht Club, and as the channel twists and turns like a serpent,
it was most useful. Jack had the binoculars out and twice got very
excited, having spotted some birds which are very rare in
England. By late morning we reached the end of the lake, and
dropped down through the lock at the end, back again to sea
level. We were now in the East Schelde which then was still
part of the sea, but under the Delta Plan is scheduled to
become an inland, freshwater lake by about 1978. The mist
was worse than ever and we crept blindly across to the north
end of the long Oosterschelde Bridge which runs some miles
across the water and has a drawbridge at its northern end. We
arrived there at 1300 hours and expected to wait until 1500
hours. But although we were the only boat, and there was a
good deal of road traffic, they opened the bridge for us and we

sailed through waving our thanks. Again we felt our way through the all-pervading mist to Colinsplaat, a fishing port on the south bank and tied up about 1500 hours.

Colinsplaat was rather a dreary town, its most interesting feature being the fish market on the quay, with large catches changing hands and going inland by lorry. Still, we spent a comfortable night in the harbour, and on Tuesday at 1030 hours left on the last passage of the cruise, 125 miles back to the Medway. Tacking with little wind but a fair tide, we cleared Walcheren by 1800 hours, passing Dutch warships at anchor, then further out saw huge lighters, some with cranes, working on the dam across the mouth of the estuary. Then on to the island of Walcheren itself where we passed a long line of deserted sand-dunes stretching to the south - our last sight of Holland. There was hardly any wind, but what there was freed to the north and we drifted onwards, being set south by the current. Next morning at 1030 hours with a fresher breeze we sighted the West Hinder lightship and raised the North Foreland by 1830 hours. A stronger, colder wind took us up the Thames estuary for a second time at night, and we strained to pick up the right buoys, giving as wide a berth as we could to the coasters and liners that came past from ahead and astern.

Again we passed Sheerness near midnight, but this time we flashed the letter Q with a torch as we sailed past the Customs Station. Again the customs launch caught us up in the lower reaches of the Medway. I never quite gathered whether they had seen our signal or not, but at least we could claim to have done the correct thing. The fact we had an American on board seemed a complication, and Bill was asked to report somewhere the following day. We anchored in the small hours near Folly Point at the entrance to the Hoo Channel. About 1100 hours on Thursday, we tried to get into the berth, but there wasn't enough water and we went aground. Another thirty minutes saw us afloat again, but with the engine not operating in neutral or reverse and with hardly any water either side of

Pussy Cat's berth, it was very awkward getting in. At one point we had to drop an anchor in some haste to prevent us being carried on to another boat, and we weren't finally tied up until 1230 hours.

I was planning already to enter *Pussy Cat* in the Crystal Trophy Race, and afterwards to take her to Malta. For the month or two before the race, it seemed worth while looking for a berth on the South Coast, and I had already made enquiries at Littlehampton, Chichester and Poole. The first two seemed to have nothing but waiting-lists, but at Poole I could get a deep-water mooring laid at Hamworthy Park for £35. Having been on a tidal mooring for nine months this seemed attractive. I had a look from the shore and decided to go ahead. The mooring man promised it would be ready before April 25. I had managed to get the gear-linkage in the outboard fixed, so I gave the Hoo yard notice of giving up my berth. Two young men, Michael and Alan, applied to come as crew on the voyage to Poole and Tokiko agreed to come and cook for us. On Saturday April 24 at 1330 hours we cast off.

When I bought *Pussy Cat* one of the features that attracted me was the fully-battened mainsail and mizzen. The sail would set better I thought when she was going to windward. The Sjöstroms had been using plastic tubing for battens, but it had a serious defect - depending on which tack you were on when you broke the battens in, the plastic tubes developed a bend one way or the other which couldn't be straightened. Thus the sail set differently on the port and starboard tacks. Also the tubing didn't fill the pockets or hold the sail as flat as it seemed it should be. The batten pockets in the sails were two-and-a-half inches wide and there were thirteen battens from 12ft 9ins to 2ft 9ins, 120 feet in total length. Wood seemed the obvious material, but a quote for shaped wooden battens at twenty pence a foot seemed expensive, and I decided to buy the wood and plane it myself. I made the battens in elm; they looked fine and were no trouble on the cruise to Holland. But now as we dropped down the Medway, something went overboard. As we turned in the moderate breeze to recover it, the boom swung over, the mainsail twisted and one of the battens cracked. As we ran along the Kent coast with a following wind the mainsail was poked forward, and as we rounded the North Foreland, another batten went. In Ramsgate harbour we shaped some spare wood to replace the broken battens, but the next day on passage to Newhaven in Force 6 or 7, all the battens in the mainsail broke. In Newhaven I had to get a complete new run of mahogany, the only wood available from a local timber-yard, and we spent half a day shaping new battens. From then on the battens became a periodic problem, and I even considered using the latest fibreglass material. However, I had a quote of between £80 and £100 for a purpose-made set, and I thought the price was exorbitant even if I could have afforded it.

We got to Ramsgate in good time, but it was low tide and there was very little water in the entrance. With her shallow draught *Pussy Cat* might have made it, but there was a keel-yacht hard aground squarely between the harbour walls, completely blocking any access. So we sailed up and down outside until 2000 hours when the tide had risen, then followed other boats in, in the dark. Once inside, trying to berth against the east wall, the engine stalled in reverse. Without thinking I pulled the cord to start it again, the motor with throttle half-open roared into life in reverse gear, the engine kicked up, broke the metal brackets that clamped it to the boat, and the whole lot half-fell into the water. We pulled it out by the controls in a matter of seconds and laid it to rest in the cockpit.

We spent Sunday in Ramsgate and by good luck, through a yacht chandler who was open on Sunday morning, found a mechanic who knew this particular engine and was prepared to come and look at it. In a matter of minutes he decided it was a long job - he would have to take the engine down, clean it, fit a new bracket, etc. I decided to leave it with him and go on under sail alone. The rest of the day we lay in the sun, worked on the battens and prepared to start with the tide in the small hours of Monday morning. We got away at 0310 hours holding a course of 160 then 190 against a south-east wind, Force 5 or 6. By 0945 hours Dungeness was in sight ahead and we were making a good passage with the wind now on the quarter behind us. But in the next few miles we lost our way.

In *Pussy Cat*'s voyages so far I haven't made much mention of the daily run, the basis of dead reckoning and all navigation. The reason is that this part of her navigation gear, the log, had one drawback. The Aga electric log which was fitted was a fine bit of equipment, sensitive, strong, well finished, carefully installed. Like most electric logs an impeller on the bottom of the boat transmitted impulses to the mechanism inside the hull, which translated them into a dialled record of speed and distance. But there was no means of clearing the impeller from inside the boat if it became fouled by weed. On any long-distance passage this seemed to happen with monotonous regularity. The merest thread was sufficient cause, and often peering under water in harbour, it was impossible to see any obstruction and one would conclude: 'This time it's something else.' But if one went back with a thin knife or a needle (a finger-nail was too thick) and cleared the tiny space between the impeller and the shaft, lo and behold, off she went.

I decided to get a Walker log (the kind that trails over the stern) as a second string, so to speak, a purchase that proved itself time and time again in voyages to come. If I were equipping another boat from scratch, I would be inclined to save the expense of an electric log. Though there are models which can be pulled through the hull and cleared, even these become fouled so often that it is a tedious business pulling them in and clearing them again and again. There is a new log on the market that can't possibly foul because it has no propeller but simply measures the speed of the water over a tiny distance along the bottom of the hull. But the cost is well over £100.

We had the new Walker log on board but for some reason hadn't streamed it, perhaps because we were too concerned with the outboard motor and the sail battens, perhaps because I just wasn't used to it. It was a lesson for us even on that short passage which we had intended should take us to Newhaven. Without an engine we had to be choosy about ports and Newhaven had a large outer harbour. We were going pretty fast with a following wind, and some time after we had passed Dungeness, perhaps about 1100 hours, Alan asked, 'Isn't that town Brighton ashore?'

'Hastings - I began. Then I wasn't sure.

We talked round it. If we had streamed the log there would have been no doubts. But when one looked at the shore - it could be Brighton. The more we talked, the more like Brighton we made it seem. Finally we decided to beat back and see if we had passed the high cliffs east of Brighton and the Newhaven breakwater. We found the weather which had been fine when following us, was not so pleasant to travel into. We all got wet and the boat banged about. Instead of cliffs, the ground got low and marshy. Finally we decided we couldn't have been so far on, turned round and ran before the wind again - but by now we had lost an hour or more and again broken half the battens in the mainsail. We hugged the coast to see if we could identify something and then saw a large sign - HASTINGS PIER! I wonder if the council put it there as a road sign for idiotic yachtsmen.

We were round Beachy Head by 1450 hours and anchored in the outer harbour at Newhaven by 1550 hours. Michael volunteered to go ashore in the dinghy and ask for a tow into the inner harbour. Mike was another excellent, knowledgeable crew member. He had come down from school after his 'A' levels, and was planning to go and work for a boat-building firm in the West Country. I had already got one free tow in Ostend, and I didn't expect another.

'Not more than £5,' I told him.

Soon Mike came rowing back in the dinghy and about the same time a launch came out of the inner harbour and chugged towards us. We gathered in Mike, threw the launch a line as they circled and they took us in tow.

'We only pay for the berth,' Mike told me. 'I think it's a pound a night.'

I recommend Newhaven Marina to any visiting yachtsmen who can get a berth there. We lay comfortably moored, with electricity and water to hand until 1530 hours on Wednesday. The facilities ashore were excellent: several good chandlers; most kinds of repairs; a club house with restaurant, bedrooms, hot baths. We paid more in Ramsgate for a less convenient, less salubrious mooring, and here they even towed us out again free, when we left on the Wednesday.

We planed new battens on the quay in the sun. We also got a local sailmaker, Captain England, to repair the pockets in the mainsail which had been damaged by the broken battens. He not only repaired the pockets, but went over the whole sail, and did the work in a day and a half. We also left with him a jib which needed a patch. Captain England, who ran his sail-loft up onthe hill single-handed, lived near in a caravan with his wife. 'Never trust the sea,' he told us. He had been captain of a sailing ship driven ashore on the Cornish coast in a storm, in the early years of the century. He showed us photographs of the wreck and some yellowing newspaper cuttings. He and his wife had been saved, but their daughter, an only child, had been drowned. It must have been forty or fifty years since it happened, yet the sorrow was still fresh in his mind 'Never trust the sea.'

On Wednesday with warmest thanks we cast off the tow at the Newhaven entrance, and set a course for the Owers lightship off Selsey Bill, course 260 degrees, log zero. At sunset I got a bearing of the sun on the horizon and compared it with the bearing given for the appropriate date and latitude in Reed's Amplitude Tables. Amplitude is the angle between the meridian of a heavenly body and its setting point and so gives a true bearing at its rising or setting. Compared with the ship's compass and allowing for variation, this is one way of checking the deviation. For most yachts, built as they are of wood or fibreglass, deviation is negligible - as it was in the case of *Pussy Cat*.

From southerly Force 4, the wind fell to nothing, and it was 0345 hours before we passed the Owers with the log reading twenty-nine miles plus. Now the wind freshened from the north-east and we decided not to turn north to Chichester, but to go directly west, south of the Isle of Wight and on to Poole. The wind backed to the north, dead on the beam and by 0600 hours on Thursday, St Catherine's Point was on the bow. It was a fresh, bright morning, the Isle of Wight looked like some green Paradise Garden and it was good to be alive. Alan and I were on deck. Alan's watch ended at 0600 hours and Mike was due to come on. Alan was a photographer from Yorkshire; he was getting good pictures with his expensive-looking camera and he didn't want to go below. On the other hand, we didn't think Mike would want to miss such a glorious morning so we compromised by calling him at 0700 hours, and I turned on a yachtsman's breakfast for the whole ship's company shortly afterwards. We surged past Saint Catherine's Head with the wind on the beam, but then we lost it, and by 1130 hours at the Fairway buoy outside the Needles we were becalmed and sweltering in the sun. Gradually a breeze came up from the south, and we picked up Poole Number One buoy at 1520 hours with seventy-six miles on the log. Once inside we picked up a temporary mooring off Poole Yacht Club and had supper together in a restaurant ashore.

I now had to find *Pussy Cat*'s new mooring. I couldn't get hold of the mooring-man that evening and it took nearly the whole of the next day, Friday, to locate him. Finally, on the telephone, he told me that it was a red-and-white buoy marked '35-foot cat' near a blue yacht called *Blue Shadow*. He would be out to help me find it that evening or Saturday morning. Alan was disappointed the cruise had ended so soon, and I offered him and Mike a day's sailing on the Saturday, but they finally decided to go on Friday evening as there were convenient trains.

On Saturday morning Tokiko and I waited for the mooring-man at our temporary berth, but getting on for 1200 hours there was still no sign of him. I was loth to start sailing round Poole Harbour with its strong tides, shorthanded, but finally we managed to get a lift from a passing work-boat that was going up towards Wareham. The mooring was easy to find; they let us pick it up and then cast off the tow. Now *Pussy Cat* was settled, we did some tidying up, rowed ashore perhaps half-a-mile in the dinghy, then parked it with other boats in the corner of a public recreation ground, hiding the oars underneath. Then laden with gear, we staggered to a bus, which took us to the train, and finally back to London.

CHAPTER NINE

CHANNEL ISLANDS, CRYSTAL TROPHY

> Bits of France thrown into the English Channel.
>
> *- Victor Hugo*

> Thou shalf not covet; but tradition
> Approves all forms of competition.
>
> *-A.H. Clough*

Poole was to be *Pussy Cat's* home until July, and I can't pretend her berth there was ideal. I joined the Poole Yacht Club as a visiting member, and that gave me a base ashore to change clothes and to keep the dinghy and the outboard safe. It was also possible, for a consideration, to get the yacht club boatmen to take me out if I had a lot of gear or it was rough. If one had to make the trip by dinghy, it was a long tedious business and if there was any sort of sea, as there usually was, the passengers and any baggage, however well wrapped, would get there soaking wet. It was a lovely spot and one could swim and enjoy the quiet and the scenery without even slipping the mooring. But it wasn't convenient, and there was another drawback.

The great power station ashore made a dramatic landmark both by day and by night. It was almost as impressive in its way as the huge pile of the Battersea Power Station on the Thames. But it filled that part of the harbour with water not polluted in any way, but *warm*. As a result the marine growth was more prolific than in most tropical waters, as I found out just before the Crystal Trophy Race.

Across the bay to Vigo, the skipper at the helm

Repairing the tiller in Saint Helier, Jersey

I had arranged the next cruise to the Channel Islands for the end of May. But it was not until the 14th that I was able to drive over to Margate (where our Ramsgate engineer had his workshop) and pick up the outboard. He was a likeable chap and he cheered me up with stories of Archimedes U40's he had known, how good they were; one he knew of had run continuously for thirty-six hours, and so on. He had been over the engine, cleaned it, got new brackets, tried it out, and he said it was all right. I got it back to the boat the same week-end but couldn't start it, finding in the end that the plug-leads were on the wrong way round. Then the following week-end when I ran the engine, I couldn't get the cooling water to come through. With the cruise only a week away repairs were urgent, but I had the greatest difficulty in getting a workshop to look at the engine. Finally one did, said the cooling water was leaking away from the water-jacket, some bolts hadn't been tightened properly and a new gasket was needed. They promised to fix it by the end of the week.

There were five of us coming on the cruise, and we were to spend ten days visiting Cherbourg and the Channel Islands. First there was Mrs Jolly (who immediately became Jo), someone who loved the sea and sailing partly because some of her happiest memories were of sailing with her husband, a naturalist, who had died about a year before. She was used to being on a boat and she took the cooking and the galley arrangements in her stride. Then there was Danny, a lorry-driver in his forties or fifties, and his son, Stephen. Danny was owner of a canal cruiser, but after some years was finding it a bit tame and monotonous, and wanted some sea experience. He was like a rock, took the rough weather with the smooth, was helpful and willing as a handyman (ably abetted by Stephen) and always good-humoured. Fourth was Peter who had been cruising (several times to the Channel Islands) in many types of boat and was thoroughly experienced. He worked for Cadburys and arrived with the latest sample packets and tins of food, to be tried out on the cruise.

Things began badly. I got down to Poole on Thursday and met Jo in the yacht club. On Friday we went ashore shopping in the morning and collected the outboard. In the afternoon Danny and Stephen came on board. On Saturday morning about 0830 hours at slack tide we cast off and went round to the Town Quay under the motor where we were to complete the shopping, meet Peter, and (perhaps) have an anchor winch fitted. It was about half-a-mile to a mile from the mooring. The engine started all right, but the cooling water still didn't seem to be running strongly enough. Then as we got round towards the quay the engine faltered and as we reached the quay it failed completely. That was the last time I tried to run it on the boat.

As we drifted past the quay, somebody appeared to take a line. it was Peter, the fourth member of the crew. The engine was very hot and we couldn't get it going again. Back at the yard there were no hands available; it was Whitsun week-end and everything was closing. They had nothing else we could hire or borrow, but they said we could use their bench and tank to work on the engine ourselves if we wanted to. Danny volunteered to have a go, but working entirely in the dark, he succeeded only in separating the top half of the engine from the bottom half, and then he was unable (like all the King's horses!) to put the two halves together again.

There seemed to be only one thing to do. I had been walking at frequent intervals past a window full of Seagull outboards. I already had the smallest size for the dinghy and it had never given any trouble. How about the largest size, the Seagull Century? We couldn't go to the Channel Islands without an engine. Certainly it would only be a quarter the horsepower of the Archimedes, but *Pussy Cat* was light enough on the water and easy to drive except against a head wind or an adverse tide. The price was £80 and after some agony I went in and agreed to buy it if it could be fitted to the boat. They brought it down after lunch and with a few modifications it worked. It was far from sophisticated. There were only neutral and forward gears. There were no remote controls and one of the crew had to crouch down out of sight to work the gear-lever and the accelerator, on code instructions from the helmsman above. It was expensive to run since it used almost as much oil as petrol, and the tiny tank on top of the fly-wheel had to be filled every twenty minutes. But it went. I kept it as a standby even after this cruise, and right to the end it went whenever it was needed, whenever somebody pulled the starting cord. That is not to say that there were not some anxious moments, when there was strong weather against us and the Seagull was not strong enough to push the boat.

We set off on Sunday at 0830 hours in wet, blustery weather and a southerly wind. Right at the start the engine almost failed us against the wind, but we managed to get sail up in time and motor-sailed to the entrance of Poole Harbour. Close-hauled on the starboard tack we passed the Needles Buoy and St Catherine's light. With the wind dead south we went about on the port tack, then again on the starboard. Gradually the wind freed to the west, but died away, and we made poor progress that night and the next morning. At 1430 hours under the motor we picked up the Basses de Renier Buoy east of Cap Levi, and tied up in Cherbourg by 1900 hours.

Cherbourg was sunny and warm. We bought duty-free wine and spirits and dined ashore in a restaurant where they greeted Peter as an old friend. For Jo it brought up past memories and when we were walking through the market in morning sunshine, a bright kaleidoscope of stalls, bustling with life, piled with fruit, blossoming with flowers, rich and gay with every kind of merchandise - she suddenly burst into tears.

'I'm sorry,' she said, 'It's just . . . we came here. I remember so vividly. I'm all right now. Isn't it lovely.'

On Wednesday we left for Alderney, away by 0530 hours with three or four other yachts, to catch the west going tidal stream. We chugged feebly through the Grande Rade or outer harbour and along the hazy outline of the coast, the wind

freshening from the north-east. By 0745 hours we sighted
Omonville then Le Hanois light. On Peter's advice we steered
somewhat to the north to allow for the tide and sighted
Quenard Lighthouse near the harbour with the wind dead
astern. By 1040 hours we brought up in Braye Harbour and
dropped anchor well in and near the sea-wall. There were
twenty or so yachts at anchor. Ashore in the dinghy, we found
a warm, rocky island of wild flowers, a sleepy town, St Anne,
with steep, narrow streets and friendly people. St Anne
seemed far less crowded with tourists shopping for duty-free
goods than St Peter Port or St Helier, and the island
generally far less commercialised. We set no anchor watch,
but I awoke at midnight with a stronger north-east wind
blowing, checked our riding light and for safety let out a bit
more anchor cable.

We had hoped to start for St Peter Port at 0800 hours on
Thursday but the north-easter was blowing dead into harbour
and we didn't fancy our chances of getting out under the
Seagull. By 1430 hours it had moderated and we decided to
try. We had buoyed the anchor and wanted to get the
anchor-buoy in first. But it was out of reach and by then the
dinghy had been stowed. However, when we shortened in to
bring the buoy nearer, the anchor broke out prematurely.
Fortunately the engine was already going, but it failed to push
us forward and we finished up alongside the sea-wall. Again
we tried and again turned against the sea-wall. A harbour
launch came across and towed us past the other yachts, while
we got the sails up. But when they cast off the tow, *Pussy Cat*
seemed very sluggish, wouldn't point up to the wind, and after
the first tack over to the east side of the harbour, we only just
went about. On the starboard tack to the north-west it became
evident we wouldn't clear the submerged end of the sea-wall,
and I tried to go about again but failed in stays. Willy nilly we
had to sail across the sunken wall and it was only sheer good
chance that there was enough water. It was quite clear
something was wrong. Then I looked over the stern and saw a

rope trailing in the water.

When the anchor broke out we had dropped back a few feet, and the float of a lobster-pot (the harbour was dotted with them) had caught round one rudder. *Pussy Cat's* rudder-blades projecting fore and aft of the stock were well balanced, but they were ideal for catching ropes, lines and under-water obstacles of all kinds. With some difficulty we cut the float loose, *Pussy Cat* kicked up her heels, and the wind, now favourable, took us down through the Swinge. We passed the lonely island of Burhou where, Peter told us, there is a solitary cottage which honeymoon couples can rent to spend the first week of their marriage as the-only-boy-and-girl-in-the-world.

Down we went towards the Little Russel Channel, anxious about time and visibility, for it was none too clear. But we had Adlard Coles' excellent pilot and Peter's previous experience to guide us, and we just made it nicely. At 1945 hours we picked up Platte Fougere on the port bow, took it to starboard and sailed on through the Little Russel past each distinctive mark - Tautenay, Roustel, Rousse, Corbette d'Amont. Peter nearly took us into Sampson Harbour by mistake, but there was Brehon Tower to take us south and eventually into St Peter Port crowded with many yachts, by 2130 hours. We had a day in Guernsey stocking up, and the crew went on various expeditions. We all met for a meal at the Old Government House Hotel with, outside the restaurant, its fine terrace and view over the town.

At 0930 hours on Saturday we left for St Helier, intending to motor out of the packed harbour and get the sails up outside. But at the entrance the engine failed to push us against a strong westerly. We began to move sideways instead of forwards, and had to turn and come in again. Barging round the harbour, followed by an anxious harbour launch, we managed to hoist the main and the mizzen leaving the jib so we could turn on either tack, and then with the engine flat out we managed to push out diagonally from the entrance. Once clear, the wind came on the beam, and we were in sight

of La Corbière Lighthouse, monumental on its great pile of
rock, by 1300 hours. We tacked along the coast and considered going into St Aubin in case the engine wouldn't get us
into St Helier. But in the bay, with smoother water and the
engine going, *Pussy Cat* pointed well and we were in alongside
the harbour wall at St Helier by 1545 hours.

During the passage one of the cleats on the mast for
belaying the main halyard came adrift. There was only one
mast-winch used for the jib, and the main halyard was worked
tight by holding the end round the cleat then pulling on the
bight above it, taking in the slack at the same time. In the past
crew had pulled outward from the side of the mast directly
against the rivets which fixed the cleat into the glassfibre.
From then on, I made it a rule that the halyard was to be
worked up by pulling from forward, at right angles to the
fixing of the cleat in the mast, and after that I never had any
more trouble.

Sunday was another day of rest in harbour. We filled the
water tanks, lugged heavy cans of petrol for miles, charged
batteries, cleaned the impeller of the Aga log, tightened up the
valves of the toilet, straightened a stanchion, washed clothes
and after all that went for a dip. Mucking about in boats can
be a full-time occupation.

On Monday it was time to start back and we cast off at 0730
hours. With north-east winds forecast, we thought of going
south and west of Guernsey clear of all obstructions. But the
wind held east, though rather light, and we decided to go up
through the Alderney Race where the tide would be running
north in our favour from 1700 to 2200 hours. Visibility was
poor for the whole passage and we saw no land from Crozier
Point on Jersey until we sighted the Needles. There was
enough wind to carry us north and just through the Race by
2130 hours. It was an extraordinary experience. One could feel
the boat being borne forward by the tremendous current, and
although the sea was perfectly smooth, there were, for mile
after mile as far as the eye could see, mysterious whirlpools

('overfalls' on the chart) in the sea. When it is rough and especially with the wind against the tide, the Alderney Race must be formidable indeed. If Charybdis and Scylla really existed, it is here one would expect to find them rather than in the sunny islands of the Mediterranean.

The wind freshened at nightfall to take us across the Channel, but fell away in the misty morning. We went too far to the west and when we sighted the Needles at 1100 hours on Tuesday, we had to beat back towards Poole. There we missed the tide, and even with the engine and a fair wind, it was like climbing uphill to get in against the force of the ebb. However, we were at the Town Quay by 1530 hours and cleared Customs.

The Crystal Trophy Race was to take *Pussy Cat* down to Plymouth which would be a good point of departure for the Mediterranean. But before then I had some week-ends on the boat and also had to settle something about the engine. Camilla, now seventeen, came down to the boat on two week-ends. The first time she brought a girl friend, Deborah. We didn't go sailing but bathed and picknicked on board. While I was working they took the dinghy and outboard for a run and buzzed off among the yachts. When they had been gone an hour I began to worry and when two hours had passed I got alarmed. They both swam; indeed Camilla brought up in the tropics was used to being in the water before she could walk. But I visualised them swept away by the tide, struggling with a water-logged dinghy, peering after a lost outboard, run down, overturned, injured. I reproached myself for not telling them to keep in view or giving them other more precise instructions. I asked several passing boats if they had seen two girls in a rubber dinghy, but I hesitated to raise an alarm. Just as well. For they then appeared rowing in good order and with hearty appetites for tea. They had run out of petrol and had to row back.

Another week-end we went from Poole to Yarmouth and

back. There was Chris who worked at Heathrow as an air mechanic and had sailed dinghies in Singapore. There was a couple from Scotland, Jesse and Ian, who had their own Bobcat and thought of coming to Malta. On Friday there were westerly gale force winds forecast and we spent the first night in South Deep, going across the bay to Yarmouth the next day at six to seven knots under jib and mizzen alone. We beat back from Yarmouth the next day, and *Pussy Cat* proved she could go to windward reasonably well in fresh weather, as she passed most of the monohulls on the same course, some of them much larger boats. It was in light airs that she did not point well as I found to my cost in the Crystal Trophy Race. Her fin keels were less trouble than a centre board, but they didn't give enough lateral resistance.

It was a good week-end. Jesse and Ian enjoyed themselves, though in the end they didn't come to Malta. Chris came along and crewed on the Crystal Trophy Race. Camilla was the most unhappy one. She had come along to do the cooking but she was seasick a lot of the time and was better when she kept out of the galley.

I had had enough of the original outboard. Following the injunction 'Always go to the top', I wrote a long letter to the managing director in Sweden, with a copy to the UK agents, telling him in some detail about my troubles and asking if he could do anything about it. I had a letter back within a week offering me a new outboard worth £350, allowing me £250 in exchange for the old one, the balance of £100 to be paid in cash. It was a generour offer and I accepted it. The new engine was to be fitted after the race when the boat was at Plymouth. It was a more powerful engine, thirty-six horsepower, but with a smaller propeller. My only worry was its extra weight, and whether it would fit on the stern.

The Crystal Trophy is an offshore race for cruising multi-hulls, and has been held since 1967. The course is from Cowes, with the start organised by the Island Sailing Club, round the

Nab Tower, across to Buoy CH 1 outside Cherbourg, then down the Channel to the Wolf Rock, round it and back to Plymouth Harbour. The distance is approximately 310 miles. I knew *Pussy Cat* wouldn't do well. She was undersailed, heavily built and we had a fair amount of gear on board. But I wanted to go in for the fun of it. I had the greatest difficulty getting her measured and in the end it wasn't properly done. The RYA very sportingly gave me a handicap to put me in the race, but with fuller information, so I was told, I would have got a better one. I had started in January in Hoo and the measurer for the Medway Yacht Club promised to do the job. After two months and several reminders he came and got the forms, but after six weeks more nothing had happened. I was leaving Hoo and I had to go and get the forms back. At Poole, after five weeks, I got the Poole Yacht Club measurer actually to come on board. He didn't take any measurements but left with a plan saying: 'I'll get it all from this, and I'll send it straight in for you.' Presumably he must have sent something to somebody as my entry for the race (£10 entry fee) was accepted, and I got my share of the finishing money which was £25.

The next difficulty I had was with crew. Peter, who had worked such wonders with the water system of the outboard and sailed so well, was my first choice, and he agreed to come. I invited Bill from the Dutch cruise because, though short-sighted, he was really keen on sailing, but I never heard from him. Then the other Peter from the Channel Island cruise, but he was involved in a family holiday. Mike, from the South Coast trip, couldn't come either. Late in the day I asked Chris, the week-ender to Yarmouth, who was pleased to join me. That made three in all, not an enormous crew for a long race, and I tried in Poole and elsewhere to get a fourth, advertising a free sail with food and drink supplied. But I had no takers.

The third difficulty I had was with the boat. There was no question of engine trouble, but there were other hazards. *Pussy Cat* had spent the winter in the mud at Hoo and come out of it with a clean bottom. I hoped that two good coats of the best racing copper would see her through the summer and out to Malta. But I had reckoned without the Poole Power Station and the warm current it created. The bottom had been clean enough for the cruise to the Channel Islands and for the two week-ends after. But then I had left her alone for three warm week-ends in June, and when I went down on a Tuesday afternoon in early July to meet the crew on Wednesday and get her ready and across to Cowes by Friday, the first thing I noticed as the dinghy came alongside were dark patches just under the waterline. I was in a bathing-suit in the next ten minutes and discovered that the whole of the bottom was covered about an inch thick with thousands of little barnacles, so close that there was hardly room to get a pin between them. I was dismayed. It might have been all right for a fish restaurant but it was hopeless for racing. Even if we couldn't repaint her, we had to scrub or scrape her clean. I rang up a boat-yard at Cowes and asked what it would cost to slip a 35-foot catamaran for a couple of hours - £40. Hmmm. I was on good terms with the boatmen at the Poole Yacht Club, and they showed me a patch of beach in the corner of a bay near the club, where we could get an anchor astern and lines ashore.

Chris, one of the crew, blessedly turned up in good time at 1000 hours on Wednesday. We got her on the beach at noon with the high tide, and between 1530 and 1700 hours we worked our backs as stiff as boards, brushing, scraping, sluicing, washing. It was a warm, sunny day. We splashed about in bathing-suits, and fortunately, except for various nooks and crannies, the barnacles, together with a good deal of the racing copper, came off as easily as wiping a slate. If the bottom was piebald at least it was clean and smooth. We got her alongside the club jetty as the tide came in about 1900 hours.

Peter turned up overnight at 0100 hours having driven down from Birmingham after work and called at several other Poole yacht clubs by mistake. As soon as he arrived we moved to a deep-water buoy and at 0345 hours on Thursday we left under the outboard with the last of the ebb. We had a good trip across and tied up to the mooring trots at Cowes by 1230 hours, having even had time to hoist the spinnaker which was brand new and had never been tried out. The scrutineering of yachts before the race didn't begin until Friday morning, and the start was not until Friday evening at 2030 hours, so we had plenty of time, and swam and bathed and drank beer ashore. However, when we enquired at the Island Sailing Club for a life-raft from Borrogear, hired for the race, it hadn't arrived.

Friday was another easy day. After a lot of telephoning and enquiry, the life-raft was found at the Yacht Club without its label but identifiable by its number. In the early evening there was a briefing supper which took some time to serve, and the start was postponed by half-an-hour. We got back to our boats about eight o'clock, moved down the river and started weaving about near the starting line. *Pussy Cat* made a good start, across the line a few seconds after the gun and well to windward (what wind there was), and if the race had been three miles instead of 300, it might have been some use to us. As it was we steadily fell back into the body of the fleet. Though we were sailing in good company, there was something a little uneasy, psychologically, about starting the race at dark. Certainly on a long cruise I prefer to start out in daylight hours and let dark come when one is used to being at sea.

Before we were out of the Solent the tide turned against us, and we made the Nab Tower with difficulty, tacking again and again in the rushing dark. Then we were round and away to the south with a good breeze now on the quarter and making up to eight knots. We had the spinnaker set but unfortunately it didn't last. This was the first spinnaker *Pussy Cat* had had, and though there was a spare pulley at the masthead and a stainless-steel halyard rove through it, the halyard was rove so as to hoist a sail on the after side of the mast not the forward side. We found it out too late to go up the mast and change it. At first it seemed all right for the halyard to ride forward round the mast, but it surprised me how quickly (in about two hours) the heavy stainless-steel wire was worn through by chafing against the mast as the head of the spinnaker bobbed about. So, long before we reached Cherbourg, the whole lot came crashing to the deck, the spinnaker tore along the foot, and we were left spinnaker-less in a race that was at least fifty percent running with the wind aft. We still passed two boats before rounding CH 1 at 1215 hours on Saturday, but thereafter on the long run down the Channel, we were passed by several boats including an Iroquois with spinnaker set and a Snow Goose with a small spinnaker. Shortly after she passed us the Snow Goose's spinnaker came down and we began to gain ground. But our hopes were short-lived for she was only changing to an enormous, blue-and-white, balloon or parachute spinnaker, twice the size of the one that had come down, and she rapidly disappeared over the horizon. All day, all night and the next day we ran and by 1930 hours on Sunday we were round the Wolf Rock, at that stage lying tenth.

There were only twenty-three boats in the race, and what surprised me was how often we were in company. During the whole three days only very rarely was there no other boat in sight, either astern or ahead. We seemed to spend all Sunday night stemming a foul tide off the Lizard and I think made a tactical error by keeping in to the land instead of standing out more, even though we would have been on a less direct route to Plymouth. Monday morning light brought to view half-a-dozen yachts all to leeward, and with a fresh northerly Force 5 or more, *Pussy Cat* held her own. But as the wind grew lighter, the other boats pointed better and moved faster. Finally with the ocean almost to ourselves, we lay becalmed for most of Sunday a few miles from Plymouth. Towards evening a faint breeze took us gradually in, past the breakwater, with fluky gusts catching now from one side now the other, and sailing up the harbour in the dark alongside *Catalpha*, another catamaran which drew ahead in the last few hundred yards. We finished seventeenth in a total entry of twenty-three, not a very good result in a fairly slow race. I could not possibly have had a better crew and Peter, in particular, didn't spare himself from start to finish to get the utmost out of the boat.

The first boat in, *Trifle*, covered the 310 miles in 55½ hours, an average of only 5.6 knots. If one compares this with some other multihull racing times the difference is striking. The record for the Crystal Trophy itself is 41½ hours, the time taken by *Trifle* in 1968, an average of 7½ knots. Going up in the scale, the record for the Newport (near Los Angeles) Ensenada (in Mexico) Race, a distance of 125 miles, is thirteen hours, an average of 9.6 knots. This was achieved in 1957 by a 46-foot catamaran, *Aikane*. The French aluminium trimaran, *Penduick IV*, in the 1969 Trans-Pac Race (she was not an official entry but sailed the course with the other boats), covered a distance of 2,225 miles in eight days, thirteen hours, an average of about 11 knots. *Penduick IV* also crossed the Atlantic west to east in December 1968 in the record time of ten-and-a-half days. *Mantua II*, a fast Australian trimaran, set up an even more impressive record for the Brisbane Gladstone Race, covering 309 miles in twenty-six hours, a remarkable average of nearly twelve knots, surely one of the fastest long runs ever made by a small yacht. Perhaps now the Transatlantic Race competitor, *Three Cheers*, is in England we will see even faster runs, since she has already broken the record for the Round-the-Island Race by covering the course of sixty-five miles in five-and-a-half hours.

Although we arrived after midnight, the secretary was there in a dinghy to meet us and direct us to a berth in Millbay Docks where we turned in and slept the clock three-quarters round. On Tuesday there were receptions and parties, meetings and discussions, a general feeling of relaxation and good fellowship. There was a civic reception at noon in the new Town Hall, an attempt by the RYA to weigh all the boats on cranes at Millbay Docks which was eventually abandoned, and an evening reception in the Royal Western Yacht Club of England. The setting was magnificent, with a wide view over

Plymouth Harbour, surely one of the loveliest harbours in England. The weather too presented us with a perfect, still evening after a hot, sunny day. Ideal weather for receptions and revelry, if not for sailing.

CHAPTER TEN

ACROSS THE BAY

> Till next day
> There she lay
> In the Bay of Biscay O!
>
> *- A. Cherry*

There was quite a lot to do to get *Pussy Cat* ready for her cruise to Malta, and I found Plymouth a better place for refitting than either Hoo or Poole. Dave the boatman of the Royal Western Yacht Club was unceasingly helpful; he not only knew everything about boats, he knew everybody in the business, and produced sailmakers, riggers, fitters, chippies and the rest, at the drop of a yachting cap. He helped me get *Pussy Cat* round to a concrete slipway where I was able to float her in at high tide, and paint the bottom while she was dried out. I had the spinnaker repaired and a new halyard rove, the right way round this time. In Cowes, one of the Admiral's Cup boats, rashly pushing out with, instead of against, the tide, had bashed the wooden bumpkin sticking out astern from *Pussy Cat's* starboard hull, which carried the QME self-steering, and I had this repaired. At least it was one item I didn't have to pay for myself. I got the batteries checked and recharged. I bought a second length of aluminium tube, and fixed spinnaker fittings either end. This was to serve for twin-running as I now had a second genoa and two forestays, so both sails could be hoisted at once. I bought a paraffin stove as a standby in case we had trouble with the gas stove.

There were four crew coming with me - Rosalie, Jane, Simon and David. Rosalie had been sailing for years in her

Alongside the Club Nautico, Vigo

parents' boat and was just as much at home on the sea as on land. Still in her twenties, she taught the piano and was learning to play the guitar. Jane was younger, still a student at Bristol University taking a degree in geology, a keen dinghy sailor but so far without any experience of cruising. But she was tough and keen and came on watch at dawn night after night without turning a hair. Simon came from a family who were enthusiastic sailors. He had done more cruising, and his brother had cut loose from his shore job to sail round the world. He was the most mechanically-minded of us, and helped more than once to repair the fuse box and get the engine of the battery charger to start. Youngest and keenest perhaps was Dave who had finished his last year at Dulwich College and seemed to have spent all his week-ends for several years dinghy sailing with the most passionate devotion. He was the best helmsman and he steered the boat as if the finishing line was half-a-mile ahead. He was always watching sails and rigging and several times his keen eye spotted a weak shackle or a chafing halyard, in time to prevent them going any further.

From the start Rosalie took charge of the provisioning and the galley, though the rest of us did the cleaning up and, on occasion, got a meal ready, perhaps something different and reasonably successful, if without the master touch. Rosalie came down to Plymouth a fortnight before we sailed and we bought most of the provisions at a big cash-and-carry whole-sale supplier right on the quay at Millbay Docks - half-a-dozen of this, a dozen of that, a ten-pound tin of marmalade, a gross of matches, a side of bacon, five-pound tin of ham, etc. etc. etc. We got duty-free liquor from a local supplier after signing various forms for the Customs, and the Customs officer came down the day before we sailed and put a seal on a padlocked cupboard, not to be opened before we were outside the famous three-mile limit. The saving on spirits was enormous; we paid something like eight bob (pre-decimal) for a bottle of Scotch; but it was much less on wine and beer and aperitifs. We took rice and potatoes but there was to be no bread-making. For one thing we only had a camp oven, for another it wouldn't be necessary. Our proposed route was Vigo, Gibraltar, Ibiza, Cagliari, Malta - and we hoped to do the longest passage in less than a week. In fact the loaves we bought at each port lasted pretty well, four or five days on average.

That week also a Penta representative came along and fitted the new engine that I had previously bought for £100. We tried it out motoring up and down inside the dock and all seemed to be well. At less than half-throttle the boat was surging along. It was about fifty pounds heavier and a job to raise and lower, but it fitted the bracket all right and it had the advantage of a rectifier which would help to charge the batteries.

On Friday night, a fortnight later, all the crew were on board. As usual there were last-minute purchases and repairs. The spinnaker with foot re-sewed was delivered on Saturday. Then came the bonded stores. We took on seventy gallons of water, six gallons of paraffin, sixteen gallons of petrol. I bought chloride tablets for the water, a new starter-cord, green and red paint to adapt hurricane-lamps as standby navigation lights (not recommended as it is impossible to keep them alight in any strong wind). One of the burners of the Primus gas stove was faulty and though we searched all over Plymouth, we couldn't find a spare burner. So we had, almost from the start, to change over to the two-burner paraffin stove and our gas bottles were never used. The paraffin stove was sometimes tricky to light, but it kept going for the whole voyage, only giving trouble after we arrived in Malta where it accidentally went on fire and nearly sent the boat up in flames.

Somehow at the last moment Rosalie hurt her thumb, and though she made light of it, we persuaded her to go and see a doctor on Saturday afternoon. She came back with it in plaster, having discovered from an X-ray diagnosis that it was broken. She assured us that she (a) hadn't done it on purpose,

(b) had been told it would be all right if she didn't use it, (c) still wanted to come on the cruise. I certainly didn't want to loose her at this stage and never regretted agreeing to let her come. She managed perfectly well in the galley, there were plenty of hands for any heavy work - not that there was very much - and Rosalie's good spirits were a tonic for everybody the whole time she was on board.

We could only leave Millbay Docks around high tide when the gates were open, and we checked that they would open for us at 0800 hours on Sunday August 8. In fact we were able to get away well before, by 0730 hours, and motored out under the engine. At 0800 hours we streamed the log and by 0830 hours we were under sail on the port tack steering 240 with the south-west wind Force 2 or 3. This sou'wester dead on the nose was an augury of things to come and for most the way, certainly until we got to Cagliari, we were close-hauled, beating into head winds. It was to be in complete contrast to the cruise from Sweden, when the wind had followed us all the way.

Soon we went about on the starboard tack steering 180, and as we got out into the Channel, we were surrounded for a time by board-bottomed ocean racers, plunging about like porpoises, beating out to the Fastnet on the last event of the Admiral's Cup. However, before long we left them behind and carried on through the first uncomfortable night. Simon and I were violently seasick. Rosalie and Dave lost their appetites. Only Jane made the transition from land to sea without a qualm.

I don't usually have such a struggle getting my sea legs, and this time I had an excuse. I wanted to see if I could make the bunks between the hulls more comfortable in a head sea by covering them with webbing raised on a wooden framework. Unfortunately I hadn't had time to do it ashore, but I had got the webbing and some wood, and I thought I would knock it up after we got under way. Knock it up! In a short steep sea pretty well any manual work becomes difficult, let alone carpentry. I managed to saw and fit the wood, but when it came to nailing anything I finally had to give up. I was lying doubled up, either on my side or upside-down. There wasn't room to swing the hammer and in any case four out of five strokes went astray due to the violent motion. Nothing would stay where it was put, either the wood or the webbing. The nails upset or danced away out of reach. Pieces of wood rolled about. I couldn't get the webbing tight. All the time I felt sicker and sicker and finally rushed up on deck and leaned over the lee of the cockpit while my stomach turned completely inside-out.

I felt no better when I went below again though I somehow finished off the job. It wasn't well done; perhaps it wasn't well thought out. It was never a success, and though, with a mattress on top, Dave slept there some nights from preference, when we got to Malta I broke it up and threw it all away. There were four good bunks in the hulls anyway, and as there was always one on watch, it was easy to switch round with our sleeping-bags in bad weather. In the very worst sort of sea, with very high, short waves, even the forward bunks in the hull were not too good. It was more like going up and down in a fair-ground amusement machine than being in a quiet, steady bedstead. Even after weeks at sea, in really bad weather, I only slept well in the after bunks which were near the centre of the boat. Only in these was one likely to echo the song: 'Rocked in the cradle of the deep, I lay me down in peace to sleep.' Also comfortable was the couch in the saloon, though there was no bunk-board to keep one in place, and it was rather in the midst of everything.

I took a meridian altitude of the sun's lower limb putting us 50° 6′ north, which with Eddystone bearing 020 degreees could be taken as about right. I took some sights later in the Bay, but at this time I was trying to work from *Reed's Almanac* which isn't very adequate for navigation and makes things difficult rather than easy. If one switches to the *Admiralty Nautical Almanac* and the three volumes of *Sight Reduction*

Tables for Air Navigation, which give solutions of the spherical triangle for all kinds of sights, then working out a sight becomes no more difficult fundamentally than looking up a railway timetable. What is necessary is to keep your finger on the right line, though even that may be tricky in a rough sea. Not having to bother with spherical triangle formulae, sines, tangents, logarithms, antilogs and the rest, is a blessed relief for those who like me are unmathematical at heart. I say this even though a good many years ago I took navigation courses and studied the fat volumes of the *Admiralty Manual of Navigation* up and down and sideways. If you must understand and know everything about navigation then there are no better or fuller treatises than the *Admiralty Manual* or *Nichol's* (not so) *Concise Guide.* If you just want to *do it* well enough to take a small, slow boat across the ocean, then the four books I've mentioned are enough, together with plenty of practice. As an introduction and explanation there are many short books and I don't pretend to know half of them. One which explains everything very clearly and is particularly good on dead reckoning and the 'sailings', is A. C. Gardner's *Navigation* in the Teach Yourself series. However, it just mentions the *'Sight Reduction Tables'* and doesn't describe their use in detail. Another book, Mary Bluett's *Celestial Navigation for Yachtsmen* deals with neither dead reckoning nor coastal navigation (though these are covered in another book), nor with traditional working-out of formulae, but confines itself entirely to a detailed description of how to take a sight, look it up ('work out' is a misnomer) in the *Admiralty Almanac* and 'Sight Reduction Tables', and plot it. This book is very condensed and needs to be read *with* the *Nautical Almanac* and the 'Tables' and combined with practical work. Nor does it give any examples for practice. However, its self-imposed limitation and concentration on one aim (to obtain a position line by the easiest method) make it of the utmost value.

However, this is by the way. The sights which I took then

and later were not entirely essential to our cruise, as our Sea-
fix radio direction finder functioned well the whole time, and
we were able to get position lines, often crossing at good
angles, whenever we needed them. In several cases (for
instance when we were making for Ibiza and Malta), there
were good radio beacons dead ahead on our plotted course.
The signal from a radio beacon gives no indication of distance
so at close quarters it can be dangerous to steer for them at
night or in poor visibility. But approaching shore is dangerous
in any case, and navigation then becomes a matter of careful
sounding, shore observation (by night or by day) taking visual
bearings and, if in doubt, *standing off*. A difficulty I find with
radio signals when they are weak or indistinct is that they
disappear over a fairly wide band of bearings, and to calculate
the centre point of this band is not easy. However, this is a
difficulty which disappears with a clear, strong signal.

Close-hauled on the starboard tack and with the wind light,
we didn't raise the French coast near Ushant until 1015 hours
on the following day. We identified Pontusval and Le Four
lighthouses and by noon, tacking to the west, sighted the
island of Ushant. Even with the tide (for a time) and the
engine lending a hand, it was a long haul to round the island,
and the turn of the tide was too imminent to risk taking the
shorter route through the Fromveur Channel. By 1800 hours
on Monday we were well west of Ushant and as the evening
wore on and night fell, and the tide which had turned against
us slackened, we gradually left the lights behind and set a
course across the Bay.

On Tuesday morning, with a light head wind, we could lay a
course of only 200 degrees, but by Tuesday evening the wind
had freshened, we were steering 230 degrees (only ten degrees
east of our best course of 240), doing six to seven knots, and
even changed from the large genoa to the working jib for the
night. We got radio bearing on Ploneis in France and Lugo in
Spain, and we experimented with a Consul grid chart.
However, it needs some practice to count the dots and dashes,

and I rather think in any case we were too far into the Bay for
it to be at its most effective. On Wednesday we were back to
light airs, at 0930 hours our dead reckoning with 330 miles on
the log was 45° 35′ north, 8° west, by radio Cabo Vilano bore
214 degrees, and a meridian altitude gave our latitude as 45°
18′ north. For a good deal of the day we drifted rather than
sailed; we bathed in 2,679 fathoms of water, and took photos
of the dolphins (or were they porpoises?) which swooped and
dived round the boat with as much enjoyment as we did
ourselves. Everybody was settling down to life on board.
Rosalie practised the guitar half-an-hour at tea-time, started
to give Jane lessons, and even coaxed the rest of us to join in
some folk singing.

That night and during Thursday the best we could steer was
between 170 and 180 degrees, and we took a tack to the west.
Then on Thursday evening at 2045 hours, with 450 miles on
the log, we sighted a lighthouse. After some discussion of the
flashes (as a marginal economy I hadn't bought the *Admiralty
Light List* thinking I could rely on the *Admiralty Pilot* and the
charts) we identified it as Punto de Peña, east of Coruña. We
lost the wind in the night, but it came back from the
south-west on Friday, a weary day of tacking to the west in a
cold wind and a bumpy sea. However, for much of the time we
handed over to the sixth 'member' of the crew, the QME
self-steering gear, and the rest of us kept snug in the saloon
out of the wind, playing cards.

There were far more ships passing and we saw many fishing
boats. There was heavy rain in the night and in the small
hours the lights of Cabo Villeano were abeam. At dawn several
fishing boats were near, and one seemed to persist in following
us though we changed course and tacked to avoid her. Before
dawn the Finisterre light had come up on the port bow. We
were now steering 180 degrees, and we passed. Finisterre, a
great, rocky cape, the Spanish Lands End, about half a mile
offshore between 0900 and 1100 hours, running for an hour
under the engine.

All Saturday afternoon there were light southerly winds, and we tacked in close to Cabo Corrubedo hoping to get a better tidal stream to help us south. Then we were obliged to use the motor to get offshore and away from some rocks to the south. There are certainly tidal streams along the Spanish and Portuguese coasts, for our progress relative to the land was far better at some times than at others in identical wind and speed conditions. The Admiralty Pilot for the West Coast of Spain and Portugal has this to say. 'Information regarding the tidal streams off the coasts of Spain and Portugal is almost entirely lacking and even what is available is conflicting. . . There must necessarily be tidal streams . . . running with considerable velocity off salient points . . . but little or nothing is known regarding them. Southward of Cabo Toriñana (north of Finisterre) the tidal streams are stated to be north-going during the rising tide and south-going during the falling tide while between Cabo Carvoeiro on the west coast of Portugal and Ilha Berlanga (near Lisbon) they are stated to be south-east-going during the rising tide and north-west-going during the falling tide. It therefore appears that the tidal streams meet and separate at some point off the coast between, but its locality is not known.' We tried to make use of the hint given in the passage, but it is hard to say with what success. The most useful aid would be a   proper tidal atlas such as is available for British coastal waters and the Channel.

At 0030 hours on Sunday the lights of Onza Island were abeam, then the Cape Silleiro light came up ahead flashing three every fifteen seconds, and at 0345 hours a high light on the Islas Cies at the entrance to Vigo. By 0600 hours when I called Jane on watch we had reached the Islands. I got the outboard down and, with the rest of the crew asleep, we motored in among wooded hills and white beaches, standing silent in the beauty of a peaceful dawn. After seven days at sea the water seemed as calm as a village pond. We motored slowly up the wide river, finding our way gradually past the commercial quays to the Club Nautico, where we tied up before noon beside the only three other yachts in the harbour. The steamer route from Plymouth to Vigo is 570 miles, but with head winds all the way, we had covered between 600 and 700 miles. On Sunday afternoon and on Monday we swam in the Club Nautico's big, fresh-water swimming-pool, replenished our water, fuel and paraffin, had two excellent meals ashore, and stocked up with bread, fresh meat, fruit and vegetables. By Tuesday, rested, refreshed and reprovisioned, we were ready to go on.

We cast off at 1215 hours and fell for the most obvious of mistakes, one I have succeeded in guarding against before and since. To lie more comfortably alongside we had tied one of our fenders to a projecting wooden pile on the quay rather than fix it on the boat. I had thought of it earlier on, but as we cast off forgot that the fender was tied ashore, not to the ship and it was left behind. Easy to get out of, it was an awkward little berth to get into, and we might have spent another half-hour collecting the fender, if somebody on the quay had not understood our shouts and signs and tossed it on board as we circled round.

Again the estuary looked most beautiful as we tacked down against the wind. Then, at the entrance, we found a high sea and a good Force 6 sou'wester dead against us. So we turned away and surging along with the wind free for the first time, ran past some nasty-looking rocks and some mysterious looking structures which might have been fish-traps, into the sheltered port of Bayona, once an ancient fortress, now a holiday resort. Here there were rather more yachts and we sailed round uncertain whether to anchor, tie up to a buoy or go alongside a pier. When we did finally anchor, Simon brailing up the mainsail with the sheet still loose, was caught unaware by a sudden gust that swung the boom over and swept him off the cabin-top into the sea, breaking a guard-wire on his way. He was all right, but he scrambled on board minus his glasses and without them he could hardly see further than the other end of a boathook. Fortunately he had another pair in reserve which lasted out the rest of the voyage. It is a point to remember when going on a long cruise, and I was to regret not carrying a spare pair of glasses myself on the cruise back from Malta.

CHAPTER ELEVEN

GIBRALTAR AND BEYOND

He had brought a large map representing the sea,
Without the least vestige of land
And the crew were much pleased when they found it to be
A map they could all understand.

'What's the good of Mercator's North Poles and Equators,
Tropics, Zones and Meridian Lines?'
So the Bellman would cry: and the crew would reply
'They are merely conventional signs!'

'Other maps are such shapes, with their islands and capes
But we've got our brave Captain to thank'
(so the crew would protest) 'that he's brought us the best
A perfect and absolute blank!'

- The Hunting of the Snark

That night we lay in our bunks listening to the wind howling down the valleys and whistling in the rigging, quite happy to put up with a night's delay. It was still blowing enough when we rounded the point on Wednesday, and *Pussy Cat* groaned and protested as she forced her way south. 'Why it's only Force 6 or so,' said Rosalie at one point, coming on deck. 'She really is a fussy old b, isn't she?' However, by nightfall the wind had moderated and on Thursday morning it veered to the west. For the first time we were on a reach and *Pussy Cat* began to move. At noon the log read 109 miles and a radio fix on Aveiro and Cape Modego put us 40° 40′ north 9° 15′ west. There was trouble with the electric circuit. Simon had already replaced two fuses which had got wet and corroded, but now it was a whole section of cable and it affected the galley, the compass light and the starboard navigation light.

By Thursday evening the wind had drawn aft and we were fairly in the Portuguese Trades running on the starboard tack. We passed Berlenga Light and the Farlihoes Light just north of Lisbon at 2200 and 2230 hours. Early Friday we passed the Cabo de Rocha and the Cabo Ransom lights and all day ran before the wind. At one point we broke four battens in the main but I had enough wood in reserve to shape new battens. Also, trying to come about to pick up a scarf which Dave had dropped overboard, we tore the spinnaker and though we sewed it as well as we could, it tore again and we had to substitute the twin-running rig. In the strong following winds we enjoyed for this brief spell, this rig worked well and I don't think we lost too much speed through not having the spinnaker. In fact we were in sight of Cape St Vincent by nightfall and Gibraltar seemed just around the corner.

That night a wild wind took us round Cape St Vincent and Cape Sagres, but gradually it died away and by noon on Saturday we were drifting, with hardly enough way to steer by, under a cloudless sky. The sun blistered down and we swam round the boat from time to time to cool down. As the familiar English stations died away on the radio we picked up some striking broadcasts from North Africa. There was singing, instrumental music and dramatic speech, some of it most beautiful to listen to and very powerful. From Spanish stations we also heard some very fine concerts, and on one occasion an English lesson cultivating impeccable upper-class accents which included this useful sentence: 'The vicar's wife is such a nice woman. We must ask her to tea.'

While we lay becalmed out of sight of land somewhere in the Bay of Cadiz, a tiny Spanish fishing boat with two young men aboard came chugging up to us and, after smiling and saying something we didn't understand, they handed us two large fish. We gave them a packet of cigarettes in exchange, which was well received. About an hour or so afterwards a much larger fishing trawler hove in sight and again offered us fish. We tried to tell them in our best English and French, with some halting Spanish words as accompaniment, that we already had fish and no more cigarettes. But they insisted, smiling courteously, and finally threw on board a large ribbon-like, silver fish nearly five feet long. It looked like an enormous eel which had had an argument with a steam-roller and it had a sharp bony nose. Whatever it was, both it and the previous lot tasted delicious and having no means of keeping them in the heat, we ate fish until we could eat no more.

On Sunday we still lay helplessly becalmed now in sight of Cadiz, and motored for an hour now and then to break the monotony. In the afternoon a breeze came from where we least wanted it - the south-east - and we tacked towards Cape Trafalgar. Cape Trafalgar light came up on the port beam in the night, and at dawn Cape Spartel light briefly appeared, then disappeared in the mist. At the mouth of the Straits, the fog was so thick we could see no land at all, and the light wind had backed to the east - again directly against us. Many fine ships passed us on the voyage, but perhaps the loveliest was the cruise-ship *Iberia,* whose simple, graceful lines appeared as if by magic out of the mist behind us, like a white princess in a fairy tale, then disappeared again ahead of us on her way to Gibraltar.

By 0800 hours we had got tired of tacking in the cloudy haze, and started the engine. By 1000 hours Tarifa Island appeared to the north, then a line of bays and headlands stretching east, and finally Gibraltar's crouching, lion-like rock. As always with the last lap when land is in sight, our progress seemed slow, but by 1500 hours we were finally at the entrance to the harbour. We had no idea where to go, but a figure on the breakwater waved us to the north, and we eventually found our way up the harbour and into the old destroyer 'pens' where we tied up alongside the quay between other yachts. Again we had had a slow passage, having covered 550 miles through the water and taken five-and-a-half days. But for the last three days becalmed it might have been different.

We were safe and comfortable in the pens, but after making enquiries ashore, found we could get fuel and water and repairs more easily at the marina which was just round the corner. So, on Tuesday, we moved round under the engine and for the first time moored by the Mediterranean stern-to-quay method. This involves putting out an anchor opposite the allotted berth then pulling back on it by reversing the engine, until the stern is near enough the quay to put out warps and a gang-plank. Mooring like this gives every yacht an easy getaway and its own gangway ashore, but it is not nearly so secure as mooring alongside, especially with the wind abeam, and it is sometimes difficult to maintain the stern exactly the right distance from the quay. In *Pussy Cat's* case there was the complication of the bumpkin for the self-steering sticking out astern, and after several ports this got so many knocks, that I had to re-fibreglass round the bolts which fixed it to the hull.

We found Gibraltar a good place to make-and-mend. There were good chandlery shops, and we got repairs done without delay and at reasonable rates. We had a whole new section of wiring put in the lighting circuit, got the torn spinnaker repaired and bought new parts for the toilet which pumped out vigorously as usual but was stubborn about pumping in and had to be flushed with a bucket. We had the batteries charged, and stocked up with water, fuel, fresh meat, bread, vegetables and fruit. I got an extra chart of Cartagena Harbour just in case we wanted to put in somewhere before Ibiza. We were given a present from another yacht of some fresh sardines. If you are ever offered fresh sardines don't be put off by the fact that they are small and not in a tin - fried or grilled, they are one of the most delicious fish dishes going.

Between jobs on the boat we had time to wander down the colourful main street and get presents at bargain prices in the crowded shops. Vigo had been very Spanish with hardly a single tourist in view. Gibraltar was cosmopolitan, a meeting-place of East and West, of Africa and Europe. Here there were Spanish nuns, senoritas with mantillas, Moroccan traders in sandals and fez, English servicemen in khaki shorts and shirts, Russian sailors with strange names on their hats, American tourists in dark glasses. We climbed the great Rock (by aerial cable car) and found high above the city another world. There were strange insects, rock plants and scrubby trees with brilliant flowers, clambering monkeys, old buildings, tunnels in the rock, mountain paths, endless stairways. And all round was the immense view and the sense of space, of hanging as it were from the sky. We looked east along the Spanish coast to Malaga, north and west to Algeciras and the big oil refineries near La Linea, south to the Atlas Mountains, and finally down to the toy houses and model boats in the harbour. Ancient travellers knew this place and its grandeur, and they called it the Pillars of Hercules.

Almost immediately after we arrived on Monday, the fickle wind had turned south and west in our favour, and I was fretting to get away. Finally at 1100 hours on Thursday the last job was done, we cast off the stern warps, hauled up the anchor, and made our way out to Europa Point, past a strange Russian research ship with three huge bowls like miniatures of Jodrell Bank, presumably radio telescopes. The wind was still in our favour and a strong westerly took *Pussy Cat* along the coast going like a train with all sail set. Gibraltar became a spot in the distance and in eleven hours we were abeam of Cape Sacratif, a hundred miles to the west.

Alas, our burst of speed was short-lived for the wind died in the night, then gradually increased from the east - as usual dead ahead. So on Friday we struggled past Adra and Almeria, then tacked south of Cabo de Gata (Cape Pussy Cat !) in heavy seas and wind now Force 6 or more. From Cabo de Gata our course was north-east and sure enough as we rounded the Cape, the wind like a fencer circling his opponent, backed to the north-east to hold us at bay.

On Saturday morning we found that an inner auxiliary

forestay from the deck to half-way up the mast had broken in the night. We then found that a stemhead fitting, a heavy bracket clamped round a fore-and-aft fibreglass beam which held the bottom of the two main forestays, had slipped back one or two inches. The main forestays had slackened off as a result, putting such a strain on the inner forestay that the stainless steel wire had broken clean through. We were able to fix the bracket firmly back into place and tighten up the two main forestays, but none of the spare rigging I carried would replace the broken stay. In the same rough weather, a heavy oval ring of stainless steel half-an-inch thick which joined the clew of the genoa to the sheet, was pulled out of shape and came loose. We replaced it with an even heavier shackle and had no further trouble.

The stay, however, remained a problem, and to get it repaired we decided to call in at Cartagena. It was on our way, I had just acquired a detailed chart, and the stop would break up what was turning out to be another slow passage. We took all Saturday and Saturday night to beat up the coast. During the night we raised Cape Tinoso light near Cartagena, but we were puzzled by a fixed red light ahead of us that showed from about 0200 hours onwards. In the morning we found it was a flame on top of a tall chimney in a petrol refinery near the entrance to the port. At 0615 hours we sighted the flashing light on Escombrera Island and tacked in to the land now visible, then motored slowly between the towering heights which guard the entrance to this Spanish stronghold, the headquarters of the Spanish navy.

Cartagena is an ancient town and the harbour lies deep between steep hills surmounted by forts with lines of century-old, battlemented walls covering the slopes below them. We tied up at a quay near the Club Nautico, and being Sunday the quay was crowded with Spanish families, bathing, chatting and lying in the sun, while the bar and restaurant were packed. However, the fish lunch was well worth waiting for. It consisted of a selection from a dozen or more sea-savouries

ranging from oysters to octopus, with a glass of white wine,
and the cost was less than fifty pence in English money.

We were berthed next to a yacht from Ireland and the
owner, Dennis, came on board for a drink. He had started
single-handed from Dublin intending, like us, to make Vigo
his first port of call. However unlike us he, starting from
further west, had no difficulty in getting round Cape
Finisterre. Indeed, on the contrary, he gave it too wide a berth.
For his navigation appears to have been somewhat haphazard,
and when he sighted the Spanish coast he had no idea whether
he was north or south of Vigo. So he chalked a notice 'VIGO'
on the vane of his self-steering gear and held it up to the next
passing fishing boat, with the arrow pointing south. They
indicated at once by signs that Vigo was the other way - north.
He had overshot the mark! So he carried on and made his first
port of call Oporto. I am afraid I kept quiet about my
experience with Hastings Pier. Now he was proceeding by very
leisurely stages up the Spanish coast, intending to winter in
San Mandrier, a port in the South of France, given a very good
mention in the *Renault Marine Guide*. We wondered ourselves about giving up going on to Malta and making for the
South of France as the indications were that the prevailing
winds (such as they were) would be against us to Ibiza and
possibly as far as Cagliari.

Cartagena was a fine-looking town, again without any
tourists. Near the sea-front there were well-kept gardens and
on display was the original of one of the earliest submarines
ever used. We managed to buy food and postcards, but repairs
were another matter. For some work on the bumpkin, the club
boatmen lent me a large auger which looked as though it
might have come out of Christopher Columbus's tool-box, but
which worked as well as the most up-to-date brace-and-bit.
But they couldn't help about the stay. None of the chandlers'
shops (*effectos navales* in Spanish) were open, so I waited until
Monday morning and armed with the broken stay and a phrase
book, went the rounds. I visited four shops and walked

half across the town before I found someone who was prepared to supply another stay (in galvanised iron as there was no stainless steel) and have eyes spliced in the end. They said they would farm the splicing out to a rigger and promised to have it ready by five o'clock. I went back early to collect it and, while I hung around, they kept looking down the road, all the time expecting (I thought) the rigger to return with the ready-spliced stay. I had been there an hour before I found that, after they took the order, it was discovered that the rigger had gone to Almeria for the day and what they were waiting for was for him to come back. Somebody had no doubt tried to explain this but my Spanish wasn't good enough to understand. There was no point wasting more time waiting, so I took the new wire, bought some wire compressors, and hurried back to the boat where we got to work at once setting up the stay by bending the wire back on itself and clamping it. We finished the job just before dark.

We were all keen to get on for it was now August 30 and Rosalie, our cook and organiser, was due to be back in England by September 7. We had covered almost 300 miles to Cartagena in three days, but there was another 200 miles to go to our next port, San Antonio in the north of Ibiza. So we left Cartagena just after dark, the lights behind us twinkling from the shore and a gentle breeze from the south wafting *Pussy Cat* past the Islote de Escombrera along the coast to the east. We turned north past Cabo de Palos in the night, but sure enough the wind backed to the north-east - again dead against us. About noon the next day we passed Torrevieja which looked from the sea (like several of the towns on this coast) like a magic city floating in the water. We went through a strait, the Freu de Tabarca between the Islote de Tabarca and the Cabo de Santa Pola, and a tide or current must have been carrying us on, for we moved far faster than was justified by the wind. By 1700 hours we were off Alicante and had to tack out to round Cabo de las Huertas. It was not until 1400 hours on Wednesday that we came up to Cabo San Antonio the jumping-off point for the Balearics. Then came our third favourable spell of wind, for it veered to the south and blew a good Force 5, so that by 1715 hours we sighted land ahead. It was the steep Vedra Island, the westernmost point of Ibiza. By 2130 hours the lighthouse near San Antonio came in sight and by midnight we rounded the breakwater and dropped anchor in three-and-a-half fathoms.

CHAPTER TWELVE

IBIZA, CAGLIARI, MALTA

> As ships, becalmed at eve, that lay
> With canvas drooping. . .
>
> *-A.H. Clough*

San Antonio was very different from our other Spanish ports. Swarming with English tourists, full of bric-a-brac shops and restaurants, one heard as much Cockney as Castilian. But we enjoyed ourselves for we hired a car (Dave being organiser and driver) and drove over to Ibiza the capital, a much older and more characterful town than San Antonio. Then we went on to Santa Eulalia where we met friends of Rosalie in a big modern hotel and then bathed from a crowded beach. We drove through farmland with almond, olive and locust-bean trees in the fields, with crops of grapes and corn, with prickly pear in the hedgerows. We had a dinner ashore to say goodbye to Rosalie with *gazpacho* and *paella* on the menu. I had intended to call at Palma, in Majorca, and possibly at Minorca too, but both Simon and Jane were worried about time, and when all the crew offered to come on as far as Sardinia if we sailed there direct, I decided to go from San Antonio to Cagliari in one single flight (if such a word can be used to describe our leisurely progress). However, we had had so much calm weather, it seemed certain that at last we would get a good wind. One thing I did do was to try and replace our troubadour-cook: I sent a telegram to Tokiko, the Japanese journalist who had been out twice before on *Pussy Cat*. She was at the Venice Film Festival, covering it for a Japanese film magazine, and I suggested she might like to go on to Cagliari and meet *Pussy Cat* there. The distance to Cagliari was about 400 miles and I estimated our date of arrival between Monday the 6th at the earliest and Friday the 10th at the latest. We were only just to make it.

In the meantime Jane took over as cook, we prepared for three, instead of two-and-a-half hour, watches at night, and on Friday August 3, at 1400 hours, we cast off (for we had moved from our anchorage to alongside the quay) and motored out into a northerly wind which shortly afterwards backed to the east. So on Friday and Saturday we made long tacks, at first north to clear Ibiza, then south to clear Majorca and Cabrera Island. Then on Sunday, Monday, Tuesday and Wednesday - four blessed days - there was practically no wind at all. We lay sweltering in the noon-day heat, the sea around us like oil, turtles basking in the sun on the surface. We could swim faster than the boat was sailing. The water was so clear we could see a little colony of striped fish that followed *Pussy Cat* for several days, and I have never seen the ocean in such pure, clear shades of blue, somehow deepening in hue as one's eye travelled down into its mysterious depths. We ran the engine in bursts of three or four hours until our fuel was reduced to emergency level, and yet we hardly seemed to have got east of Minorca. For a time Jane was sick and the rest of us shared watches and managed the cooking. It was not until 2000 hours on Thursday that we sighted San Pietro light in Sardinia bearing 160. We were north of our course as we expected, and turned south to work our way round to the Gulf of Cagliari.

For the first time we were short of some provisions - fresh fruit and vegetables, fruit drinks and coffee - and had to stop washing clothes and dishes and ourselves in fresh water. Then at last, on Friday, the wind freed to the west and we began to move fast again. Near the south of Sardinia we went between several islands - Il Toro (the Bull) on one hand and Vacca (Cow) and Vitello (Calf) on the other. We set the spinnaker, steadily the wind increased and going up into the

On board. Marina Piccolo, Cagliari, Sardinia

Stern to quay in Malta. Looking from Manoel Island to Sleima

Gulf we were surfing down the crests of the waves at fifteen
knots and more. It was a struggle when we came to lower the
spinnaker and I got a rope burn, losing the skin off the back of
my hand in the process. Then, using the big winch we
managed to get it in without any other damage. By 1800
hours on Friday we were tied up in Cagliari Harbour, dead
beat. We had taken over seven days to get there, an average of
about three-and-a-half knots, but we had covered the last
eighty miles in six-and-a-half hours, an average speed of over
twelve knots.

I went ashore and managed to buy some fresh fruit, cheese,
bread and butter, and brought them back to the boat. After
our shortage of fresh food it was as good as dinner at the Ritz.
Next morning, Saturday, Jane and Simon went off to book air
passages. Dave, intrigued by the atmosphere of Sardinia,
went to collect travel brochures, while I went in search of
Tokiko. There were no messages in the port, but at the *poste
restante* counter in the main post-office there was a hotel
name and a telephone number. I took a taxi and in half-an-
hour Tokiko was telling me what a wait she had had. She had
arrived on Tuesday, and found that there were no less than
four yacht clubs and marinas. But there was no sign of *Pussy
Cat* at any of them either on Tuesday or Wednesday or
Thursday or Friday. She was in fact running short of money so
she intended giving up on Saturday and going back to
England. We had arrived just in time.

On Friday night all we could find was a rather poor berth in
the commercial port. There was building going on all around
with clouds of dust, and it was a balancing feat to get ashore.
On her recommendation I looked at the Marina Piccolo, a
delightful spot though a mile or so out of town, and decided to
move there. Then we went back to *Pussy Cat* and all had lunch
together. Jane and Simon left after lunch to catch their plane
and Dave came round with us to the marina, about five miles
by sea round Cape St Elia. Dave then left in the afternoon with
plans to make his way back by train and ferry overland.

That very afternoon in the marina a young man stopped and asked where we were from. 'From Plymouth bound for Malta,' I told him. 'Would you like to have a look round?' I showed him over the boat and he was duly impressed. I told him I was looking for someone to come on to Malta as crew just in case he might know of somebody. There was no response at the time, but that evening he came back himself and offered to come. He wanted help with his return passage and I promised to think it over. He was a Belgian called Paul, one of a family of twelve; he had been in the Congo, and now he was working on a farm outside Cagliari with his older brother, planning eventually to buy land himself. He had done some cruising in the North Sea and wanted to get a boat of his own. Apart from anything else, it would be better to take Paul than an Italian because of the language. I spoke French reasonably well, and Paul's English was quite good. At the same time it had happened so quickly, I didn't think I could count on him, or should wait around for him, and I went ahead with preparations as if we were going to make the passage on our own.

So the next morning we started to walk to the tram hoping to find a shop where we could stock up. It was something of a forlorn hope for it was Sunday and we had been told everything would be shut. We had hardly got outside the marina when an Italian I had talked to on the Saturday stopped and offered us a life. His name was Simi and he had a little fishing boat berthed in the marina. His English was about as good as my Italian, but somehow we managed to tell hime what we wanted. He then picked up a friend of his, Massa, and they drove us miles to a little grocery shop that was doing a roaring Sunday trade. They helped me translate in the shop, then took us on to Massa's house where he presented us with fresh eggs, a bottle of his own wine, and a cup of coffee. Then they drove us round Cagliari and back to the boat where I showed them round and we had a drink. While we were there Paul came back and helped us to interpret.

When the two Sardinians left, Paul stayed for lunch and in the afternoon drove us out to his brother's farm, past mountains of salt from the salt-pans which surround the town, along dusty country roads, past lush farms dependent on irrigation, over low scrub-covered hills, to the rough clay bungalow where he and his brother lived in not very comfortable conditions. There we met his brother, a big quiet man who spoke no English but careful, courteous French, and had tea. By the time we got back to the boat we were all good friends and it was agreed Paul should come. Then in the evening to crown the day, Massa and Simi came back with bunches of grapes and other fruit as a present, and we all sat round until late, eating and drinking and talking.

When we got away at 0900 hours on Monday, with dark clouds and a shower of rain, the westerly that had taken us into Cagliari was still blowing, and we made good progress, first with the spinnaker set then with the genoa. We lost the wind in the night, but still by 0800 hours on Tuesday there was a hundred miles on the log. Paul proved extremely handy and quite tireless. He shared with us some food and drink he had brought: a goatskin bag of dark-red Sardinian wine, strong but with an excellent flavour, and some flat pancakes of shepherds' bread which also tasted very good.

On Tuesday morning the wind got up from the south-east - dead ahead again! Hauling in the sheets, the best course we could make was due east towards Sicily. It was the sirocco, hot and humid, and when in the evening there came another shower of rain, it brought little trickles of red dust like blood down the mast. An hour later the wind died, then started to blow again harder than ever from the north-east right on the beam. All night we careered through the pitch black darkness at ten to twelve knots, absolutely on course for Malta. We passed near only one trawler so there was no shipping to worry about, but all the same by morning I had had enough of surging forward at speed, not able to see where we were going.

By Wednesday, when the wind fell light again, with over 200 miles on the log, Pantellaria came up abeam, a dim shape about ten miles to starboard, and Malta lay less than 100 miles ahead. On thursday at 1445 hours, with a light following wind, we sighted Gozo our final landfall, dead ahead.

At first we planned to put into Gozo for the night, but we were moving at only two or three knots, lazily rippling towards our journey's end in the evening sunshine, and it was dark before we got in under the land. Gozo harbour is on one side of a narrow, rock-strewn strait and no lights were shown on the chart. The wind was increasing. Valetta was another twenty-five miles away. It seemed best to stand off, heave to, and go in comfortably in the morning. We put the boat on the port tack heading away from the land, lowered the mainsail and hove to under mizzen and genoa. Then, as the genoa was pressing uncomfortably against the shrouds and cross-trees, we changed it for the working jib. It was providential that we did so.

The wind was by now blowing hard from the north-east and steadily increased, but the boat lay comfortably and the lights of Malta spread out behind us, made comforting company. Then about 0200 hours it really started. A great storm was on its way, and the thunderous orchestra came nearer and nearer. By 0300 hours the lightning flashes were running into one another so that outside it was like a ghastly, artificial daylight. The howl of the wind mingled with the roar of the thunder and the rain poured down in torrents. From dozing on watch I had come fully, uneasily awake, and Paul and Tokiko who had been asleep came up out of their bunks. We all put on lifejackets and sat in the saloon. My mouth felt suddenly dry and I drank a glass of water. The wind we found afterwards reached a good Force 12, officially recorded on shore as over seventy-five miles an hour. Looking out from the cabin in the glaring light, the rain and spray seemed to be travelling horizontally, and the seething sea was blown almost flat by the wind. The boat was rocking, shaken by the blast, and the masts shivered. The battens in the mizzen were smashed by the force of the wind and the batten-pockets torn. A flap with the maker's name was torn clean off the jib. There was nothing to be done, and we simply sat there without talking, struck silent by the force and grandeur of the storm. At the same time I felt a surge of satisfaction that *Pussy Cat* was taking it in her stride.

After about another hour, with thankful hearts, we felt the fury subsiding. It was quieter, the rain was lighter, the flashes fewer and further away. Out on deck the lights of the island though somewhat obscured by bad visibility, seemed to be relatively in the same place. Tokiko and Paul retired again and I lay down on the couch in the saloon to wait for morning.

Soon after first light we started in. Moving crabwise in the night, we had made a few miles away from the land and Valettta was about twenty miles distant. The leech of the mizzen lacking battens, hung like a dish-cloth, but with a moderate beam wind we made fair progress. By mid-morning we were off the entrance, but then our new outboard refused to go (due as we found later to the plugs) and we changed it for the Seagull. We turned aside from the entrance to the Grand Harbour, and then more by good luck chose the middle of the three arms (Sliema, Gzira and Msida) which lie on either side of Manoel Island. We were helped to a convenient berth by Malta Yacht Services, and by noon on Friday September 17, tied stern to quay 100 from the Government Yachting Centre, within walking distance of shops and the Yacht Club. *Pussy Cat* had been twenty-nine days at sea, twelve days in port and had covered some 2,500 miles.

CHAPTER THIRTEEN

RETURN JOURNEY, TRAPANI AND PORTO CERVO

> I must have liberty
> Withal, as large a charter as the wind,
> To blow on whom I please.
>
> *- As You Like It*

When I got to Malta, I decided to put *Pussy Cat* up for sale. She had proved her strength and endurance at sea, in harbour she had the accommodation of two or three luxury caravans, and for sailing round the world one might have done worse. But she was infuriatingly slow in light airs, she wasn't easy to manoeuvre short-handed for coastal work, the business of pounding in a sea was tedious on long passages, and the big outboard was a problem to handle. She was both more and less than I wanted.

But I wasn't prepared for divorce at any price. In many ways she could be altered and refitted without enormous cost. If I got enough of my money back, to get another good boat, well and good. If she didn't go - that would be all right too. I put her in the hands of one agent in Malta, one in the South of France and three in England and advertised her in the multihull journal, *Multihull International*. But for nearly a year I didn't have a single enquiry. Then two people wrote from Germany. One was a German who wanted me to sail her to Spain (to a delightful port where he had a villa) for him to look at, but wouldn't contribute even £10 to the expenses of the voyage. The other was an American who changed his mind a fortnight later. I decided that Malta was a better place to buy a yacht than to sell one. Berthing and maintenance are

Lifting out for the winter in Malta

Up the hill to Pussy Cat's winter berth on Manoel Island

good and cheaper than England and it is English-speaking, so consequently Malta attracts yachts, whose owners make the effort to get out there. They then seem to find it a more difficult business to get their boat back to England. Thus there are usually yachts for sale. On the other hand, the number of local buyers is small and for interested buyers in England or Europe, it is quite an undertaking to go out there and see a boat. So in 1972 I set up a cruise back to England, this time sailing via Sicily, Sardinia, Corsica (I hoped) and by canal across France, from Sète to Bordeaux.

But first I had to settle *Pussy Cat* for the winter. We spent a pleasant fortnight getting various jobs done, enjoying the sun and the sea and making excursions by bus to different parts of the island. One quickly made friends with other boat-owners whose craft were moored nearby. Particularly friendly were Dorothy and Dennis, living on a beautifully-kept, luxurious motor-sailing Oceanic catamaran with powerful diesels in both hulls. After warm farewells, Paul left by air to go back to Sardinia. The best arrangement for *Pussy Cat* seemed to be to have her hoisted out and stored on 'the football field' behind the Manoel Island Yacht Yard's premises. I could have left her in the water, but both the cost and the risks would have been greater. In the harbours round Manoel, there is a constant scend of the sea which pushes yachts continually to and from the quay. In a storm there is considerable risk of the yacht dragging or breaking moorings and hitting the quay, and constant supervision is necessary.

Some of the Maltese firms I dealt with were slow and inefficient, but the Manoel Yacht Yard was very good. The yachtsman could command the wide resources of a big commercial yard, get the benefit of competitive commercial rates, and yet receive individual and careful attention for even the smallest job. Their quote for winter storage was half that of two others, yet I am sure *Pussy Cat* was looked after better than she would have been elsewhere. When the time came to take her ashore, we floated her into a little dock that was just big enough to hold her. Then a mobile hoist drove, with its wheels either side of the dock, over the top of her, and she was lifted with heavy slings under bow and stern. Slowly the hoist drove up the hill, and *Pussy Cat* took her place in the rows of yachts waiting for next season. We spent the last night on board as if we were in the Ark on top of Mount Ararat, and the next day took the ferry and train back through Syracuse, Messina, Naples, Rome, Genoa and Paris to London.

I made the same journey the other way round in the middle of the following July. Much less comfortably, as from Rome there were no sleepers to be had on the train, and I spent the night sitting in a crowded carriage, weary-eyed and over-warm, and then had a twelve-hour wait for the ferry in Syracuse. Still the market there was gay and colourful, the ferry when it arrived was airy and uncrowded, and when I got on board late on Monday evening *Pussy Cat* was still high on the hill, none the worse for her exile ashore, except that the sand driven by winter winds had taken the bloom off all the varnish, as if it had been rubbed with sandpaper.

One of the crew was already on board, having hitch-hiked out the week before. This was Pete, an American student, whose home was in Michigan, on a lake where they were able to enjoy ice-yachting in winter and water-yachting in summer. He was a tall, well-built, elegant-looking hippy with beautifully-kept long hair, and he often wore a band round his head to keep it in place, making him look like an American Indian. I remember enjoying an exchange between him and a French lock-keeper at one tiny village we passed through by canal. The Frenchman knew one or two words of English and was trying to break through the barrier and make some contact with what was a strange, outlandish phenomenon in this remote corner of La Belle France.

'Where from?' he asked.

'America,' Pete replied.

'Indian? Wa-wa-wa-wa-wa! Schwittt. . .' The Frenchman went through the sounds and motions of an Indian war-cry and shooting an arrow.

'No. Not Indian,' Pete shook his head.

'Non? Where from?'

'Chicago,' said Pete, his lake being not very far away from that celebrated town.

'Aaah. . .' I am sure the lock-keeper was pleased that if his first American visitor didn't fall into one movie stereotype, he clearly fell into the other.

'Aaah. Chicago. Gangster! Bang-bang-bang-bang-bang.' And in a rapidly-improvised mime he cheerfully mowed us all down.

The rest of the crew joined us at the end of the week - Penny, Brian, Roger, Richard and Keith. Penny was the only girl. She had finished school and was on her way to a Welsh university to study marine biology. She was very much the outdoor type, not so keen on cooking (as I had hoped since someone had said she was a good, plain cook) as on taking watch and sailing the boat. However, there were plenty of hands and we took it in turn to do the honours. Brian was the most experienced of us all and a cook into the bargain. He had trained on HMS *Worcester* and spent ten years in the Merchant Navy. After seven years in the film business he had a yen to go down to the sea again, and had fixed up three summer cruises. His first cruise had been from England to Gibraltar as one of the crew on a large, luxury twin-screw diesel-yacht, his second from Gibraltar to Sicily helping with the delivery to the Eastern Mediterranean of a new British-built fishing trawler. Now he was coming back with *Pussy Cat* from Malta to Plymouth. When he arrived he regaled us with stories of high life on the diesel-yacht and low life on the trawler. His kedgeree was a most popular dish and his chartwork was careful and accurate. Roger's business was in computers, but he was a keen dinghy sailor and he loved the sea. I remember after a day and a night and a day pounding into a short sea in the Channel with a Force 7 wind sending spray into the cockpit, most of us wet and cold and weary, he took the helm with a delighted smile and said to me - 'This is grand, isn't it?' Richard and Keith arrived together by train. Richard was with Leylands and Keith was a photographer. They were both dinghy sailors, Richard with more experience, and while he was with us Richard was the man with the engine. Unfortunately they both had a limited holiday, and we knew it was on the cards they would have to leave before the end of the cruise.

Before we sailed we had a disaster with the Penta 36-horse-power outboard. The local agent who had laid it up for the winter, sent it down with a fitter to fix and test it. He got it on the bracket and in the water and started it on full throttle. Then intending to throttle down, but mistaking the gear lever for the accelerator, he put it at full speed into reverse! There was a tremendous racket, the engine kicked up, the wooden bracket that held it to the boat cracked, and it fell half into the water. It was out in ten seconds, the fitter full of apologies and the engine was taken ashore and tested and a new iron-and-wood bracket made. The agent assured me all was well, but as the cruise went on the engine gave more and more trouble, and when it was overhauled in England, it turned out that water sucked in through the air-intake had hit one cylinder-head, bent a piston, put out the crankshaft and affected the timing. It says something for the engine that it went as long and as well as it did.

The last of the crew, Penny and Roger, arrived on Sunday night, and we cast off on Monday at 1430 hours, having completed all the jobs in the morning, and got on board the last fresh fruit and vegetables. Provisioning was good in Malta, prices were reasonable and we bought everything at one shop, getting a fair discount on the bill. We made one mistake in buying an almond syrup to mix with water which was so sweet and sickly that nobody would drink it. Duty-free stores were available but we avoided Maltese wine which

seems to have deteriorated in quality, perhaps because they try
to produce it in excessive quantity.

We motored out of the harbour and started beating north
on the port tack against the prevailing nor'wester. Our first
stop was Trapani at the western end of Sicily, looking out on
the Egadi Islands. The distance was only 190 miles, but we
were to have a slow passage with light and head winds. What
made matters worse was that we had fog for four nights
running and well into the day. According to the pilot this thick
fog is peculiar to Southern Sicily, since fog is almost unknown
in the rest of the Mediterranean. It persisted even with Force 2
or 3 winds and even five knots is unnerving in zero visibility.
Fortunately there was little shipping and except for one fishing
boat, the foghorns we heard sounded reassuringly distant.

We first sighted misty shore lights at 0305 hours on
Wednesday with eighty miles on the log, probably the town of
Gela. Then it was a matter of tacking along the coast, making
slow progress and often worried by poor visibility on the
inshore tack. We passed Licata at 1205 hours on Wednesday
where we identified the lighthouse building from the description in the pilot. In a clear patch we picked up Cape Rosello
light at 0500 hours on Thursday bearing L29, then at 1158
hours passed Sciacca. At dusk on Thursday we were in the bay
east of Cape Granitola, and, without realising it, sailed into
the middle of almost fifty small fishing boats with nets. There
we got in a complete muddle, not knowing whether the nets
were between the boats (or which boats) or behind the boats,
or at one side (or which side). They were beginning to show
lights but we had no idea what they meant - if indeed they
meant anything more than just to show there was a boat there.
They waved and called in Italian but we had no idea what that
meant either. It was as if we were caught in a net ourselves. To
make it more difficult, there was not enough wind to
manoeuvre. Finally we started the engine, and after turning
three complete circles, amid much conflicting advice from the
crew, we finally escaped without I think causing any damage.

That night we felt our way round Cape Granitola and up north, sighting Port Marsala and the Egadi Islands as the fog gradually cleared, at 1020 hours on Friday. By 1300 hours we had motored into Trapani and tied up in blazing heat and a dead calm. It had taken us nearly four days, an average run of only fifty miles a day. Trapani is an old, picturesque fishing town, the port dominated by a towering statue of the Virgin and Child. We were the only yacht, comfortably berthed alongside a quay not far from the main street. There was water and fuel near the quay, several ships' chandlers, and authentic, cheap and unpretentious restaurants.

We had chosen Trapani on the advice of Denham's *Tyrrhenian Sea* which recommends the excursion to Erice. Denham's books are such attractive Mediterranean guides, it is a pity they are going out of date because so much development is taking place so quickly. At any rate Erice is still there, and a most delightful excursion. We took a bus, then climbed by aerial cable-car to around 1,000 feet, out of the dust and heat of sea-level, to an ancient Greek-temple site, where Ulysses is supposed to have called on his meandering cruise from Troy back to Ithaca - considerably off course. The first thing we saw was the lovely, early-Renaissance church. There were fine gardens and a high Norman tower with dramatic, plunging views all round the horizon. We wandered about enjoying the coolness and greenery, and ate delicious lemon ice-creams.

Our next stop was to be Porto Cervo in North Sardinia, 270 miles distant. Richard and Keith were afraid we might have another slow passage which would make them late, and they left us on Saturday morning to take a plane. However, when I came on deck at 0070 hours on Sunday to rouse the others and get ready to sail, there they were on the quay looking disconsolate. They had been charged exhorbitant fares for taxis, failed to get seats on the plane, and after an uncomfortable night, had decided to take a chance and come on with us to Sardinia.

Malta to Trapani, Sicily. Richard from Birmingham and Pete from Wisconsin

Roger in the dinghy, Porto Cervo

Luckily the wind had gone round to the south, and we reached out of the harbour and ran north-west first on one tack then on the other. We lowered the spinnaker before dark, there was change in the air, a falling glass, lightning in the sky and rain on its way. In one of the flashes at midnight Roger swore that the stay between the two masts glowed green and crackled in the supercharged atmosphere. The wind gradually veered west and increased, by 0200 hours it was pouring with rain and by 0400 hours the wind was up to Force 7 or 8. For a couple of hours we lowered the mainsail, reaching more easily under jib and mizzen.

Due to the bad weather I had an accident with my glasses. As it was too wet to see with them on, I put them on the chart-table, and someone, no doubt due to a lurch of the ship, must have put their hand on them and had broken one of the lenses. I cabled to England from Porto Cervo, but didn't get a replacement until we arrived at Bordeaux. I could see without them but could not read or do chart work, and it was a big handicap.

On Monday morning, with a fresh north-west wind and rising glass, we were close-hauled on the port tack, still more or less on course. By evening we were reaching in light, variable westerlies. We had curry for supper and Brian, who had been brought up in India, entertained us with an account of his first sailing voyage, aged seven, along an irrigation canal in a converted bath-tub!

On Tuesday we saw a red sunset, little wind and 183 miles on the log. From noon a southerly wind, light but increasing, carried us northward. There was a suggestion of land in the clouds to the west and at 1740 hours we sighted high land, possibly behind Cape Comino. At dusk there was an outline far ahead which we reckoned was Tavolara Island. Again the wind veered north and we spent the night and the next day, Wednesday, tacking up the coast, a dramatic, rocky landscape dominated by the crags of Isola Tavolara which rises 1,800 feet almost straight out of the sea.

It was not until 1830 hours that we were off the entrance to Porto Cervo. The wind by then was due west, and the entrance looked so narrow I didn't think we could possibly get in under sail. At the same time the engine was giving trouble and Richard, who had been working on it, confessed himself baffled though he thought it might take us in. So we tried it, got almost past the entrance, and then when it failed we would most likely have gone on the rocks or had to sail out again if a motor-boat had not taken a line and towed us to an anchorage to the north of the harbour. On the south side there were boats lying alongside, but a big ocean race was in the offing and the berths were all taken up by large racing-yachts.

The first time we dropped anchor it dragged and came up choked with weed. But this time we had room to sail and we tacked up the harbour to anchor again in ten feet on a sandy bottom. We put out six fathoms of chain and rope from the port bow to the main Meon or Daneforth anchor, and carried a Fisherman anchor with rather more line but no chain, out from the starboard bow by dinghy. The Mistral was blowing a good Force 6, and as a precaution we kept anchor watches throughout the night. By morning the wind seemed certainly no stronger, and the crew went ashore before lunch, leaving me alone on board. They had plenty to do. Richard and Keith were due in England on August 7 and it was now the 3rd, so they had to find out about air passages. We needed fresh fruit, vegetables, bread, milk, meat, a mechanic for the engine, petrol, oil, kerosene, bottle-gas.

As the day wore on the wind got up stronger and stronger. The yachts in the international regatta (Italian, French, English, American, Japanese), with mainsails reafed to pocket-handkerchiefs and tiny storm jibs, scudded on their beam ends up and down the harbour until it was decided to postpone the scheduled race for a later date. I was increasingly nervous about *Pussy Cat,* but there was not much I could do. She was bucking and kicking and swinging almost through ninety degrees to the two anchors. The starboard cable of nylon did its best to chafe through and I bound it with tape, then a length of hose. I would have liked to veer more cable on the main port anchor but was afraid of the strain it would bring on the weaker starboard side. In retrospect, it was perhaps a mistake to have had anchors from both bows, for the swing of the boat may well have eased and pulled each anchor alternately in the soft sand of the bottom. By 1630 hours I measured gusts up to Force 10 and then in one particularly wild, screaming blow, the port anchor dragged, then the starboard, and *Pussy Cat* began to drift towards the entrance.

CHAPTER FOURTEEN

RESCUED BY CORSAIRS

Ships are but boards, sailors but men; there be
land-rats and water-rats, land-thieves and water-thieves.
- Merchant of Venice

Immediately I was driving down on a 1,000-ton motor-launch,
but as I prepared to fend off, I quickly saw it as a haven rather
than a hazard, and before I drifted past got a line taken and
secured. Unfortunately it was the short end of the starboad
anchor-rope and, as the port side was nearest the launch, it
held *Pussy Cat* out at an angle of sixty or seventy degrees into
the wind. I got another line across to them, but somehow they
failed to secure it. I had time to hoist both anchors, but then
the first line parted as it was bound to do, and I was on my way
again. An Italian from the launch (at least I suppose he was
an Italian - he looked dark and handsome and spoke no
English) had come on board to help me, and as we drifted
away I thought I had recruited a hand. But then to my
disappointment he dived overboard without saying goodbye,
and swam back to his own boat.

The rocks at either side of the entrance were now very near
and the engine of course was out of commission. The sails
were bent on, but the jib had at least six ties on it, and as I
started to undo them I saw I would never get it free soon
enough. I rushed into the cabin for a knife, cut the ties and
got the jib hoisted just in time by a few yards to steer *Pussy Cat*
out through the entrance. Once outside, with time to breathe, I
got the jib better set and the mizzen hoisted, and tried to sail
under jib and mizzen. Unfortunately the large genoa rather
than the working jib had been bent on and I couldn't get her

Drinks ashore at the Heine's. Ralph, Penny, Christian, Pete, Roger

Martin Heine and a friend on the rocks, Porto Cervo

to go about or drive up to windward. I was too tired by then to set about changing the jib at once, and I was being driven further and further from the shore.

Several racing yachts sailed past, but they had their own problems, and I got curious looks rather than offers of help. I came near to what I thought at first was only a racing mark, then near the buoy I saw a large, grey object. As I looked closer I saw it was a rock. I remembered it then on the chart to the north of the entrance, and was thankful that by good fortune I would clear it without difficulty. At this point three boats came out of the harbour and straight towards me - a small fishing boat with a slow, powerful engine; a rubber rescue-boat with a big outboard; and a smart runabout launch.

Worrying about separation from the crew, as much as any immediate problems affecting *Pussy Cat,* I was in a mood to accept help. I had some idea of the danger of letting people on board or accepting a tow with their rope without bargaining first, but the circumstances and my lack of Italian made this almost impossible. Two Italians in the rubber boat came alongside, then on board, and while I steered, they got a line to the fishing boat which slowly towed me back inside. In about half-an-hour they took *Pussy Cat* to the very head of the harbour with a line ashore and an anchor from the stern.

Then the head of the gang, who had directed operations from his launch, came aboard, and as he spoke good English I was able to thank him, offer him a drink, and ask him how much I owed him. He put me off, saying he would have to talk to his crew, and asked me to go ashore with him and make a statement of what had happened at the coastguard office. My own crew were on board by now, and I found they had seen *Pussy Cat* drifting towards the entrance, and had gone to the coastguard station for help. As there was no coastguard launch and we were not in the regatta (otherwise the launch that took a line as we came in might have helped), the request had been telephoned to Signor Branca of Sub and Sea Sports as his visiting card had it.

Branca kept asking me about the insurance of the yacht, and the next day, Friday August 4, having said goodbye to Richard and Keith, I went with Roger to Branca's house, and telephoned the insurance brokers from there. Branca seemed to know the telephone operators and booked calls through two channels to expedite matters. With my lack of Italian, I doubt if I would have got through at all from the public telephone in the town. When the call was booked I pressed him again to say what he wanted for towing *Pussy Cat* into harbour.

'What do you think it is worth?' he asked.

'Oooh . . . about £100,' I suggested.

'I am claiming £2,500,' he told me. In fact his claim went to court at £3,500.

It was a curious situation. The calls took a long time, Roger left to do some shopping, and I found myself politely having lunch with Branca and his household. There was a pleasant older woman, bilingual in Italian and English and in charge of the catering, and a younger woman on holiday from New York who knew the film and publishing world. She was apparently catching a plane to America the next day, after some weeks in Porto Cervo. We talked about Italian films, music, goggle-fishing, multihulls, farming in New Zealand, living in London and New York, modern painting, drugs and the younger generation.

It was an elegant setting. A cool, white, stone-and-tile house with sun-deck, and a fine view out through the harbour entrance to the open sea. Branca showed me some of his treasures from skin-diving expeditions - Greek and Roman amphora and statues, coral and marine fossils, one of which he claimed was millions of years old. He had travelled all round the world, knew most European countries and went every year to the Red Sea on under-water expeditions. We drank dark, strong wine from his father's vineyard, apparently not far away in Northern Sardinia. We ate antipasto, local salad, cold meats, cheese, trifle and fruit. Branca assured me he didn't want to cause me any trouble, but he didn't see why the insurance company shouldn't pay. He had been fighting a French insurance company over a similar claim for two years now. This time he was determined not to have the same difficulty

Finally, at three in the afternoon, I got a call through to the claims manager in London. He said they were sending a telex message to Genoa for a local representative who would advise and assist me. It says a lot for London insurance that by ten o'clock on the same evening, I was talking to Doctor Sardo, Lloyd's agent from Olbia, a largish port twenty miles away. We sat in the piazza, the centre of Porto Cervo, glamorous as a film-set, surrounded by elegant shops and looking down to the boats on the water.

'Branca is crazy,' said Sardo in French, tapping his head. 'His claim is ridiculous. Don't worry, tomorrow we will fix this up and you can leave.'

But 'tomorrow' Saturday, at eleven in the morning, Branca's launch came roaring across the harbour and three people came on board - Branca himself, very short but strong and athletic; a big, heavily-built lawyer; and a shrimp-like, diminutive clerk of the court. The latter two might well have come out of one of Donizetti's operas. I offered them a drink but they had more serious business than sitting around sipping beer. Under the supervision of the other two, the clerk of the court served me a writ half-a-mile long holding *Pussy Cat* (valued at £12,000, more than twice what I had paid for her three years before!) as security for Branca's claim. They asked me to sign an undertaking to observe the order, otherwise they would put a policeman on board, and after some demur I did so. They stressed the word *penale* in the section about infringing the order.

'That means you will go to prison,' said Branca agreeably.

Later on Saturday, I gathered that the insurance company had offered Branca a million lire (about £750) in settlement, but he had turned it down. Apart from the claim, life went on.

On Saturday evening there was a reception in the piazza for
Princess Margaret, but no one on board wanted to go. A
disloyal lot - or perhaps they just felt they didn't have their
dinner-jackets. On Sunday morning Penny's Highland blood
boiled over, and she set off alone determined to climb a rocky
peak, about 2,000 feet high overlooking the harbour. She
didn't get back until after two in the afternoon, having had a
bad time contending with acres of thickset thorn bushes, but I
gathered she got to the top, or very nearly to the top.

We had been moored just off some elegant villas with their
own beach, and we went ashore and asked the occupants of
one if we could get a hose to a tap and take some fresh water
to fill the tanks. They were an extremely friendly and helpful
German couple, Irmgarde and Christian, with three young
children. They came on board for drinks with the kids, who
had great fun racing along the deck, down the fore hatch,
back through the cabins and along the deck again. . . On
Sunday we all went in their car to a Sardinian country
restaurant in the hills, where they served an enormous hors
d'oeuvre with a choice of 100 dishes at least, and to follow,
among other courses, suckling-pig and country sausages
roast on a spit over a roaring wood fire. They were indignant
about Branca's claim, said I should complain to the manager
of the Consortium, and also suggested (as did several others)
that we should slip away at night.

We also learned from them more about Porto Cervo,
managed by its Consortium of wealthy villa owners under the
Aga Khan. It was certainly beautiful, there wasn't even an
orange peel in the harbour, but as any untidy operations like
workshops or boat-yards were carefully restricted, the
facilities for visiting yachts wanting work done were practically non-existent. The only mechanic in the place worked
for Branca. At every meeting I had with Branca, with Sardo,
with anyone, I stressed the long journey we had in front of us,
and our urgent need to get on. I also kept asking Branca, time
after time, to send his mechanic to service our engine, and he

kept promising he would do so. There was talk of the insurance company making a deposit which would release the boat, and on Sunday I wrote a cross note to Branca, with a copy to Sardo, saying the boat had been grossly over-valued, that the insurance company was making a deposit, would certainly meet its obligations, and I didn't see why I should be kept kicking about Porto Cervo, while opposing parties argued in court over an exorbitant claim.

On Monday, about lunch-time, Branca's mechanic came out and, surprisingly, got the engine going rather well. But I could get no news from Sardo all day, though I hung about until I was tired of waiting hoping he would call. Then in the evening, when I got him on the telephone, all he could say was that a new firm in Milan were handling the affair. It was a comfort having an ally, but I couldn't help feeling that Sardo was not nearly as efficient or forceful as Branca. I went back to the boat on Monday evening depressed and undecided. We had already lost four days we could ill afford, the crew were losing their morale, and if we left now they might still have to leave before the end of the cruise.

We had talked about going at night and Brian had carefully plotted courses through the Straits of Bonifacio. The wind had turned from west to east and would be in our favour once we got outside. We had the engine fixed, temporarily at least. I had no qualms of conscience about going. Branca was in effect holding me to ransom, and even with three boats and five men, even allowing for a degree of danger, even if my £100 was too low, an hour's work was worth only about a fifth of what he was claiming. I was grateful for his assistance, I wanted to see him fairly paid, but being under duress was another matter. On the other hand if we didn't get clear away. . . Any encounter either with one of Branca's boats or any official craft, would be more than embarrassing. Instead of being inconvenienced, I would be in serious trouble.

But by 2000 hours I had firmly decided to take a chance. There was no moon and we were on the far side of the port.

Porto Cervo. Buoying the line ashore prior to our moonlight flit

Our friends ashore knew we were going and put their house lights out. At 2200 hours, when it was quite dark, we slipped Branca's anchor rope and buoyed it, then motored out at half-speed. Once outside we went full ahead and hoisted the sails as well. There was not much wind, but the engine kept going without a hitch. The shorter route lay south of Caprera, Maddalena and Spargi Islands, but it was all within Italian waters, and instead we went north along the Corsican coast. We were beyond the three-mile limit by 2300 hours. By 0030 hours we were north of the main channel, the Bocca Grande, and turned west through a narrow pass between Lavezzi Island and the Lavezzi Rock on the Corsican side. Brian was on deck most of the night, checking lights and bearings, and alterations of course. We were through the pass by 0200 hours and by dawn were past Cape Feno, well up the Corsican coast and on course for Sète with a fair wind. At 1000 hours I was called up from a nap in the cabin to look at a warship that came up behind us . . . but she was a US cruiser on manoeuvres.

I called the insurance company when I got back to London and they were relieved to hear from me. I think they were quite happy I had gone, but they said Branca could have had me arrested in France or for that matter in England. They asked me for a statement of what happened. I took it in to them and discussed the affair, and they decided that the next move was up to Branca. They were sticking to their original offer of a million lire. I learned that in salvage claims there is no cut-and-dried formula either based on the value of the vessel or on anything else. Everything depends on the circumstances, on what the parties agree or the court decides.

For weeks I heard nothing, then in the middle of November, after I had sold *Pussy Cat,* I had a phone call from Branca who was in London. He had tried to see the insurance people but they had referred him to me. I met him briefly at the Naval Club. He was with another girl, Italian this time but speaking perfect English. He told me in a friendly way that breaking bail had put me in the wrong, and if I ever went back to Italy I would be arrested. To help him I rang up the insurance company and got them to arrange a meeting. At first I was to be present, and then they decided they didn't need me. And so far as I was concerned that was the end of the affair. I gathered that Branca got more than their original offer, something over £1,000. No doubt he threatened to go ahead with legal proceedings and they reckoned it wasn't worth the time and expense fighting him. It doesn't seem to have affected my insurance status adversely. I lost my no-claim bonus, but I would have done that whatever the amount. And recently they have agreed to cover me for a much longer cruise, half-way round the world, at a rate which by comparison with others seems very reasonable.

CHAPTER FIFTEEN

THROUGH THE CANALS

Open, locks
Whoever knocks.

- Macbeth

Tuesday and Wednesday saw us nearly across to the Gulf of
Lyons with good winds, and we sighted Porquerolles light
before dawn on Thursday. Many times on the cruises to and
from Malta we had seen dolphins, but on this passage, for the
first time, we came near two schools of whales. On the first
occasion they were some distance off, but the second time
they were all round the boat, and one whale surfaced only a
few yards away. It was as if a grey island had suddenly
appeared in the waves, which gave a vast sigh, then a great
spout of air and water. It would be serious if one came up right
under the boat, and there are quite a few accounts of small
boats being damaged by big fish. One should be able to guard
against the boat hitting a rock, but if the rock comes and hits
the boat, there is not much one can do about it! I believe the
silence of a sailing boat can be a danger if there are whales
about, as it may seem just another big fish, and it is advisable
to start the engine and the echo-sounder. In any case I
suppose the chances are far less than being involved in an air
crash or an accident on the M1 and these are risks we all take
quite cheerfully.

On Thursday and Friday we lost the wind. We motored a
little. We went through an oil slick which made a mess of the
topsides. There was a gorgeous sunset in the evening, not
much colour in the sky for there were no clouds, but the most

vivid and varied greens and greys and purples in the sea itself.
By 1100 hours on Friday, with 360 miles on the log and about
forty miles more to Sète, the wind backed to the north-west
and we were sailing close-hauled. Late in the day we sighted
land ahead and also to the north, and decided that Sète lay to
the north. The northerly wind was falling in any case, so we
motored north, and by 1930 hours tied up opposite the
Customs House. The town was crowded and gay with French
holidaymakers, the quays lined with fishing boats, the streets
packed with fish stalls and fish restaurants. We had arrived at
the beginning of four days' public holiday and we were to have
more trouble, this time with our permit for the canals.

I had applied for the permit at the French tourist office in
London at the beginning of July, and they promised it would
be sent to me, addressed care of the Customs House (*La
Douane*) in Sète. We had the right address since I had passed
it on to the crew to use for personal mail and there was a letter
waiting for Penny. We could have got a permit, starting from
scratch, simply by applying to the Départément des Ponts et
Chausées (Roads and Bridges) at Sète, but by Saturday it was
already shut. The Customs themselves had no authority to
issue a permit, but they were as helpful as they could be, and
said it would be all right if we went on to Beziers, thirty
miles and eight locks away, where we would find a branch
office to give us a permit.

After a luxury breakfast of fresh bread and butter, eggs and
coffee with fresh milk, we moved across to the Yacht Club
(Société Maritime), in the south-west corner of the harbour,
where we got the two masts taken down by crane in less than
an hour and for thirty francs, at that time under £3. At a fish
stall, we lunched on fish pies, prawns, *moules* and *escargots de
mer* (digging them out of their heavily-scrolled richly-
decorated shells), washed down with white wine. Then at 1600
hours, after a last-minute purchase of mosquito-netting and
elastic to cover the four hatches in case of need, we set off. We
had to wait for the swing bridges out of Sète, then motored

Going uphill in the Canal de Midi, near Beziers

Peaceful nights under the trees, Canal de Midi

through the shallow, calm water of the Etang de Thau, into the Canal de Midi, through the first lock, and tied up for the night by a grassy bank under tall trees. Delightful peace after wakeful nights on the ocean swell.

The next morning we were up at 0600 hours and started through the half-dozen locks to Beziers. There was no travelling at night because the locks closed promptly at 1930 hours every evening and were open for traffic again just as punctually at 0630 hours every morning. There was nothing to stop a boat carrying on to the next lock, but then it had to tie up and wait for the lock to open the following morning. Though all the locks were manned and the lock-keeper, male or female, took charge of the operation and did much of the work, it was the accepted thing that the boat's crew all helped. Indeed it would have been a very slow business otherwise. We also found that it made a difference whether the lock was in our favour or not - that is whether it was waiting ready for us to float in and be lifted either up or down, or whether we had to wait for the gates to be closed, the lock filled or emptied and the gates opened again, before we could motor in. In theory, if another boat was travelling the same way ahead of us all the locks would be against us. But often the lock-keeper would wait, so several small boats could go through together. And sometimes a boat coming the other way would tip the scales in our favour. We only suffered long delay on one occasion, when a barge was in a lock for several hours, using it as a dry-dock to change its propeller.

One or two lock-keepers asked us for our permit, but when we said we were getting one at Beziers, they let us go through without question. We arrived there at 1100 hours and were referred to Monsieur Siffre, in an office down the road, for our permit. But his office and his house nearby were closed, and the neighbours told us he had left about an hour before, had gone on holiday fishing, and wouldn't be back until Wednesday morning. The lock-keeper was adamant in refusing to let us go on.

'Even if I let you go, the others would not,' he said. 'I have no authority.'

He suggested we should make the best of it and join in the holiday events - bull-fighting, dancing, carnival - up in the town. But it was now August 13. Peter was booked on a plane to the States in early September. Roger had a dinghy-sailing date in Cowes. Penny wanted a few days at home before going to university. And both Brian and I had to get back to our businesses in a reasonable time. If it wasn't a race round the world in eighty days, it was a slog back to Plymouth by the last week in August.

Roger was the most enterprising, and persuaded me to walk into town with him to try the Syndicat d'Initiative. It was shut. But while I bought Sunday cakes, Roger hung about and by some miracle caught the director, Monsieur Albert Nicolau, coming out. Though he was organising a bull-fight at two in the afternoon and a grand ball in the evening, he had time for our problems. He drove us back to the lock, had a long talk to the lock-keeper, drove us miles up the canal to two further canal officials, and finally got us a 'provisional' permit, as far as Toulouse, from the Chief Engineer of the Midi Canal. There we would have to apply again for a permit to cover the rest of the way to Bordeaux. He was a friend indeed. When I sent him a letter and a present of some chocolates from England, he wrote thanking me: 'Cet échange de bons procédés est un symbole de la parfaite entente qui peut régner entre les personnes de nationalité différente lorsque la bonne volonté existe de part et d'autre.' Francophils and franco-phobes please note that we have one friend at least in France.

So on we went, up a double lock and over a high aqueduct with a sweeping view of Beziers and its cathedral on the hill opposite. Then came a series of nine locks together, fortunately worked by electricity rather than by hand. These lifted us up a steep slope and at the top a tunnel took us through the remainder of the hill. On and on we went, always climbing - Sunday, Monday, Tuesday. We passed Poilhes,

Roubia, La Redorte, Trebes, Carcassonne, Villesquelande, Bram, Castelnaudry. Carcassonne was the most famous city with its medieval fortifications, though the canal passes by on the other side, through the new town.

We were having more and more trouble with the engine. It wouldn't start, it went unevenly, the water didn't circulate, it stopped in a lock. Sometimes we had to haul the boat along by hand and twice as a result we went aground, on the shallow sides of the undredged canal. A Frenchman gave us a tow for quite a long way to Carcassonne. But there were the compensations of regular sleep every night, beautiful scenery, the fresh food we could buy at the locks and in the villages. Often the lock-keepers' cottages were real homes with kitchen gardens, hens, rabbits, children and gossiping groups. Sometimes they were just shelters, manned by day and deserted after closing hours.

On Tuesday the weather was threatening and on Wednesday it was miserable, steadily raining for hours, cold and with the wind in our faces, a day worthy of England at its worst rather than Provence in August. The Penta chose this lowest point to give up entirely. We had pulled the starter cord so often that finally we broke a little plastic arm whose point caught in some teeth on top of the fly-wheel and turned it to start the engine. We tried to file the plastic down to form a new point but it was impossible. We needed a new part. With some misgivings we took off the 36-horsepower, three-cylinder job and substituted the six-horsepower, one cylinder Seagull. But though we dropped speed between locks from five-and-a-half to three-and-a-half knots, we went steadily on and had no further trouble.

Four locks beyond Castelnaudry we reached the highest point, 620 feet above sea-level, and began to go down. In canal cruising downhill is easier and the difference is not just psychological. Uphill you enter an empty, high-sided lock liable to scrape the widest part of the hull. The lock fills with great spouts, surges and whirlpools, the boat bucks and swings like a restive horse and may crash against the side, any current through weirs or canals at the side is against you. Going down you float with more clearance at water-level into the lock. The water goes down calm and dignified, and your exit from the lock is helped by any slight flow of water there may be. There are occasionally, I believe, locks narrower at the bottom than at the top and one has to push the boat out from the side as the water goes down. But they cannot be very common and there were none on the canals we passed through.

On we went to Toulouse, passing Segala, Gardouch and Montgiscard, and at 1600 hours on Thursday we tied up in the middle of the third largest town in France. The weather was fine and the locks were all in our favour. As soon as we arrived I went ashore and at last got a regular permit which would see us through to Bordeaux. The main offices of the two canals, the Midi and the Garonne, were only fifty yards from our berth, and the permit was issued without question. I expect they knew all about us anyway. Roger tried hard to organise repairs for the Penta, but August is the month of *fermeture annuelle* and the best we could do was to get a local agent to ring Paris and get them to send two of the little plastic arms for the hand-start by express to arrive the next day. So as not to loose any time, we were to leave at 0600 hours on Friday and Roger was to wait and catch us up by train or bus to Montauban on the Friday night. In the evening we explored the centre of Toulouse, found a workmen's restaurant and tried their five-franc menu. It really wasn't bad, much better than other meals we had ashore at three times the price.

At Toulouse we had come to the end of the Canal de Midi, and the next morning after going through various basins, and taking one or two wrong turnings (for there were no road signs), we found ourselves in Le Canal Latéral à la Garonne, which would take us the rest of the way across France. Each of the two canals has its own character. The Midi, never straight, winds among hills, through cuttings, along slopes,

Canal viaduct near the River Garonne, Roger directing

Bordeaux Yacht Club. Masts just stepped by the crane at rear

across gulleys. The Canal Latéral marches in long, straight lines down a wide river valley in many stretches as far as the eye can see, and goes sometimes alone, sometimes running alongside or crossing the great river. Both are tree-lined with high elms, oaks, beeches, planes, mimosas or firs, providing shade and holding the banks. Both run through farming country of pear, peach and apple orchards, through crops of tobacco, Indian corn, aubergine and melons, through vineyards and meadows with cows and sheep grazing.

Under dull skies and drizzling rain, past Fenouillet, St Jory, Grisolles and Dieupental, we arrived at Montech, and realised that Montauban, where we had arranged to meet Roger, was on a separate branch canal, ten miles long. There seemed no point in making a twenty-mile detour, which might only have confused matters, so we stayed put, and Roger turned up after all at 2200 hours that night. He had worked out where we must be, and hitch-hiked from Montauban. However, though he had waited for two deliveries and even besieged the post-office (to considerable effect I am certain) the starter parts had failed to turn up.

The next day was Saturday August 19 and we had been a week in the canals. For my part it could have gone on and on, but we were nearing the end. We passed through Montech, Castelsarrasin and Moissac, a beautiful old town where, more than any other place, I would have liked to stay and explore. We passed the last lock before Agen just at 1900 hours then motored on in the dark until we reached the town quite late. There we had a meal ashore of the local *cassoulet* and *vin rosé*. Early Sunday morning, past Agen, we dropped down a series of five locks, while behind us the rising sun and mist on the water formed a picturesque prelude to a hot, cloudless day. The outboard droned on and on, day after day, without a stutter. If it was heavy on oil, we probably used less petrol because of our reduced speed. Now through banks of purple-feathered reeds, it was only forty-nine miles to the last lock and then forty miles down river to Bordeaux. That evening

Early morning mist. The canal needed dredging near the bank

when we moored I walked across to the Garonne and looked at the racing current that would soon be carrying us to the sea. We reached the last lock, Castets-en-Dorth, at 0845 hours on Monday. High tide at Bordeaux was at 0446 hours and low tide at 1259 hours, so the current would be with us for at least three hours. But we had no chart of the river, and one lock-keeper said to us: 'Wait for high tide, especially at this season. Unless you know it, the river is dangerous.' However, the lock-keeper at Castets reassured us: 'It is not so difficult. You should keep always to the embankment side, where the bank is built up with big stones. Avoid always the side with shingle-banks.' He was nearest the canal, so we decided not to delay but to follow his advice, and we came safely through to Bordeaux.

Out into the river, tide and current helping, *Pussy Cat* swept along on the broad stream at a rate of some eight knots, like a prisoner suddenly free and running for life. There was an instant dramatic change from the days of quiet, confined canal to the wide, turbulent flood of the Garonne. It was a different, grander, more expansive world. Now it was Monday August 21 and time was getting short. We carried the tide half-way to Bordeaux, but as soon as it turned the weakness of the Seagull became apparent, and at 1400 hours we had to anchor. Then a fat, friendly barge laden with gravel and an even fatter bargee, came by and, in response to our signs, gave us a tow. For two hours we followed their wake until they berthed a couple of miles short of the Yacht Club, in a *Modern-Times* setting of clanking cranes, conveyor-belts, hoppers and crushers - a mechanical bedlam by the riverside. We pressed a bottle of gin on the bargee which he was loth to accept, waited another twenty minutes until slack water and in another hour were nosing into the Bordeaux Yacht Club moorings. There the boats are secured fore-and-aft on metal arms to hold them against the never-ending current (there is hardly any stand of the tide) flowing fiercely either upstream or down. The club is miles out of town, and neither fuel (the

nearest garage being shut for August) nor provisions, nor
chandlery, nor repairs, were readily available. Also I am sure
there is still mail waiting for us there, though we gave the
rather cheerless couple who ran the place a pound to send
anything on. However, we got water on the quay, and the masts
were put up again for forty francs.

I invited on board a Frenchman who seemed interested in
the boat, and he became friendly. Monsieur Robert had done
the cruise round to Gibraltar and back again via the canals.
He worked in Bordeaux but though he belonged to the
Bordeaux Yacht Club, he lived and kept his boat in Arcachon,
a big land-locked harbour twenty miles to the south. He took
us into town in his car, and we had an excellent meal in a
Chinese restaurant which he recommended. Then we all went
back to the boat with him, and sat late round a bottle.

CHAPTER SIXTEEN

HOME AND FAREWELL

> Oh! dream of joy! is this indeed
> The lighthouse top I see?
> Is this the hill? is this the kirk?
> Is this mine own countree?
>
> *- The Ancient Mariner*

We spent Tuesday stocking up, getting the masts stepped and rigged and preparing for sea. There were battens, sails, water, petrol, oil, stores to be got ready or bought. We took off the festoons of fenders adjusted the stays and shrouds, checked the halyards, laced up the sheets, tried the winches. Baths in the Yacht Club were five francs a time which the crew thought expensive, so we hosed ourselves down on the quay as we had done once or twice in the canals. With not much time to spare we caught the tide at 1815 hours and dropped down river, close-hauled against a northerly breeze and without enough room to sail properly. We picked up the BBC weather forecast which gave easterly winds for Biscay, but locally they were more from the north. However, with the engine and tide helping more than the sails, we made five knots, though the Seagull was quite unhappy in some reaches where the wind against the tide gave us a short, choppy sea. We carried on down river until 0030 hours when the tide started to turn against us, and dropped anchor out of the channel on a mud-bank in the centre opposite the sizeable town of Pauillac, about half-way to Royan at the mouth. This passage down river in the twilight and then in the dark was one of the strangest of the cruise. It was quite unlike the sea, yet in some

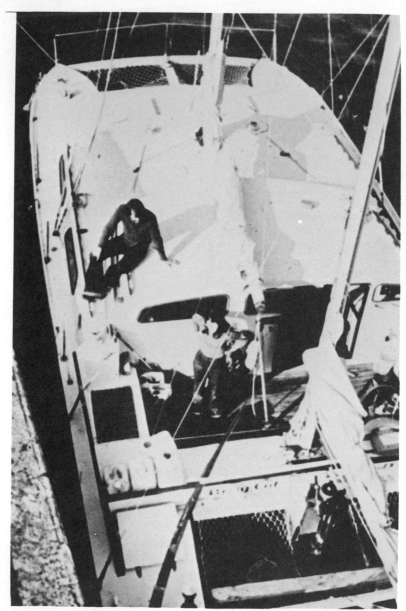

Last view. New owners on board at Millbay Docks

places, especially after the Dordogne joined the Garonne and the two together became the Gironde, it was wide enough to loose one bank or the other. There was a wild, lonely, eerie feeling about it, but whether it was the place, or the time or the occasion, is hard to say.

Up again at 0530 hours we hoisted the anchor and were under way by 0600 hours. By now the wind had freed to the east enough for us to sail down the channel close-hauled. What a relief! Making at least another two or three knots under sail, we hauled up the Seagull, laid it to rest with the Penta in the cockpit, and didn't use it again until we went into Millbay Docks at Plymouth.

By 0945 hours we were at the entrance opposite Royan, clear of tides, and cut across, past a clattering crowd of dredgers, to the tall, nodding buoys of the Grande Passe de l'Ouest. There was a feeling of freedom and release in being at sea again and with deep water under the keel. We streamed the log and took our departure from Buoy 1A at 1100 hours with an easterly beam wind, on course for Ushant. By dark we had lost the coast. Penny made a large risotto for supper and, back to sea routine, we set watches for the night. All Thursday a favourable easterly carried us across the Bay on a reach, our fastest and most comfortable point of sailing. At 2200 hours we sighted the Ile de Seine light and at 0230 hours on Friday morning, the Ushant light. But the wind was backing and as we rounded Ushant close-hauled it was too far north for us to lay Plymouth.

Crossing the Channel the seas got steeper and more uncomfortable. A radio-fix put us on a course which would take us to the coast between Lands End and the Lizard, making some allowance for tides and leeway. Then at 1925 hours we sighted the Lizard on the starboard bow. At 2000 hours we went about on the port tack course 130 degrees, taking the steep swell head on. The boat was bumping badly and all night we struggled, wet and weary, seemingly getting little nearer our goal. Dawn brought lowering skies and a blustery sea, but we

were able to point north, 020 degrees on the starboard tack.
With the high seas and Force 7 wind, *Pussy Cat,* usually a dry
boat, was swept by showers of spray and some solid water, and
it was sodden work at the helm. Gradually as we strove north
the buffeting of the seas eased. We never saw Eddystone, but
by 1430 hours we sighted land east of Looe and tacked close to
the shore towards Rame Head. By 1530 hours we were in the
Sound and at 1640 hours we picked up a visitors' buoy off the
Royal Western Yacht Club of England.

On the voyage home from Malta, we had covered about
two-thirds the distance sailed on the outward passage, and it
had taken some ten days less. We had covered in all 1,750
miles, had been thirty-two days at sea, eight-and-a-half days
in port and, in addition, nine days in the canals. Our last meal
together was fish and chips in a dockside cafe, but we still had
sea appetites, and they were all the better for being home
again.

It was time to say goodbye to *Pussy Cat.* Whereas the year
before when she had been in Malta nobody wanted to know
about her, now there were half-a-dozen people interested.
One prospective buyer with his son (very keen) and his wife
(not so keen) had been on board at Malta before we sailed.
Another cabled to me care of the Yacht Club at Bordeaux.
Now she was lying at Millbay Docks, three people came to
look over her. Still she wasn't sold yet and, before I left
Plymouth, I moved her to a berth at Foss Quay, a little spur of
land on an arm of the sea south of Tor Point, where there were a
number of other catamarans and trimarans. It was less
convenient but cheaper for a long stay, and it was a beautiful
spot.

I had not been back in London long before the agents rang
up and asked if a prospective buyer from South Africa could
go down and look over *Pussy Cat.* He saw her during the week,
was full of enthusiasm and asked if I could meet him and his
wife on the boat at the week-end. Jane and I drove down on

Friday night arriving after dark in the pouring rain and with the road to Foss Quay under six inches of water. It was blowing hard, *Pussy Cat* was straining at her moorings, and we were soaked and almost had to swim to get on board.

I had a disturbed night, but when the prospective buyers, Johann and Alicia, arrived after lunch on Saturday, the weather was lovely and stayed so for the rest of the week-end. I planned to move *Pussy Cat* back to Millbay Docks on the Sunday. It would give Johann a chance to try her out under sail and motor, it would be easier to arrange a survey, and it would be more convenient for him if he decided to buy her. He and his wife had come from South Africa to buy a boat. They wanted something they could live on over the winter, learn to handle and then sail back to Cape Town. They had looked at monohulls and multihulls, trimarans and catamarans, and this was what they wanted. On Saturday we went across by ferry to arrange for the berth. We talked to Dave who was as helpful as ever, and then came back and spent the night on board. On Sunday morning, with a northerly breeze, we sailed up and down the harbour several times trying her out on all points of sailing, and after two or three hours, motored into Millbay. Johann and Alicia were delighted and asked me if they could take her over there and then, move in and make her their home. I came down the following week-end when the survey had been satisfactorily completed and took off a few personal belongings. That was the last I saw of *Pussy Cat*.

It is always a wrench parting with a boat, and I miss *Pussy Cat* in many ways. When I was in Holmsund after I had decided to go ahead with the purchase, Erland said, 'You won't regret buying her.' And indeed he was right. Buying a boat brings worry, trouble and expense. But it brings other things as well. It brings the need to learn varied and interesting skills and the satisfaction of using them. It brings the need to organise and anticipate. It brings too the enjoyment of changing natural scenery, the stars and the moon at night, the

sun at dawn and dusk. It brings the enjoyment of exercise in
the open air and the pleasure of meeting and swapping yarns
with other enthusiasts of all ages, classes and nationalities. It
satisfies man's urge to go on journeys, to plan the means and
the route, to manage hazards and adventures on the way, and
to achieve a safe homecoming at the end. Finally it gives the
pleasure of meeting a challenge from the sea and the weather
that everyone can temper to their own ability and experience.

INDEX

INDEX